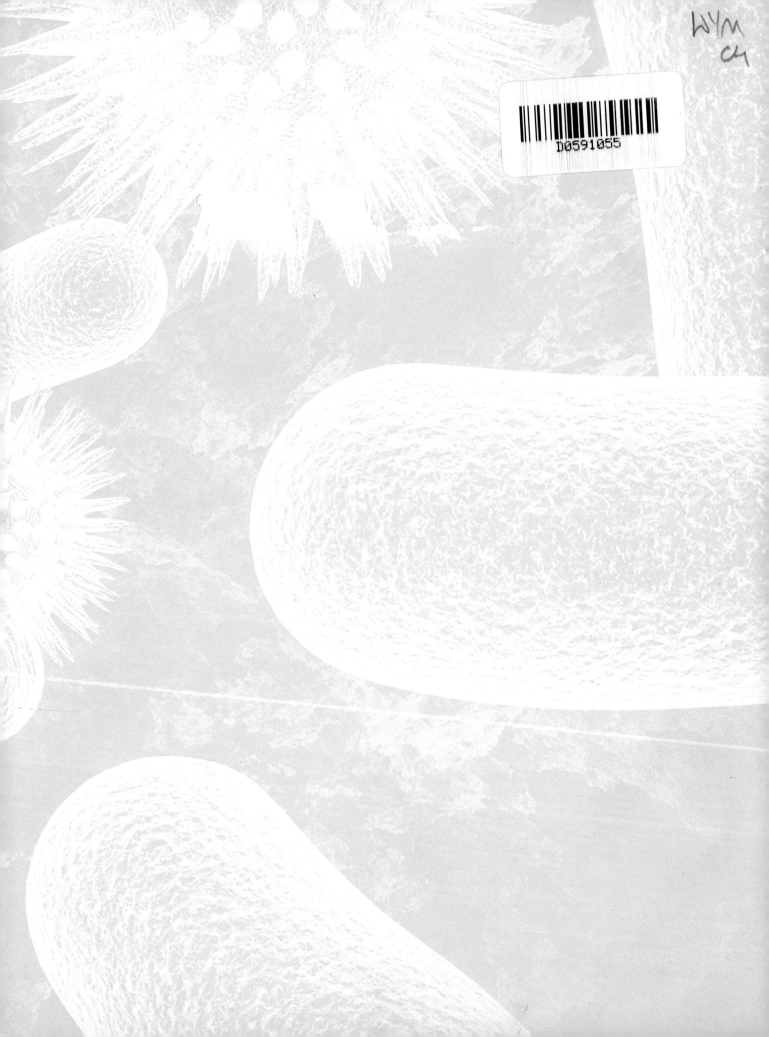

Do You Know About?
Science

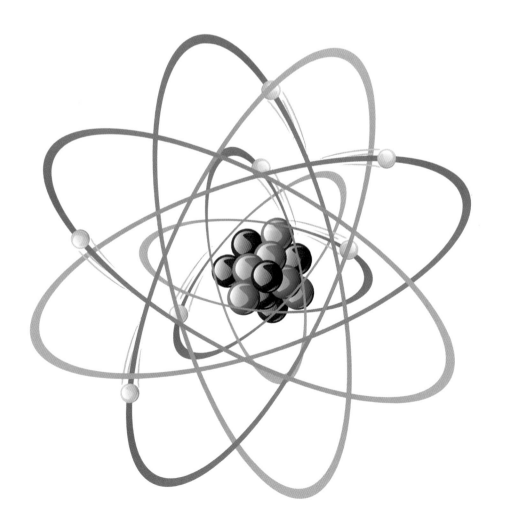

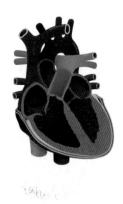

Do You Know About?
Science

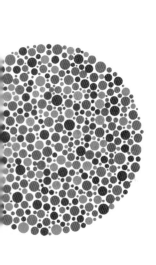
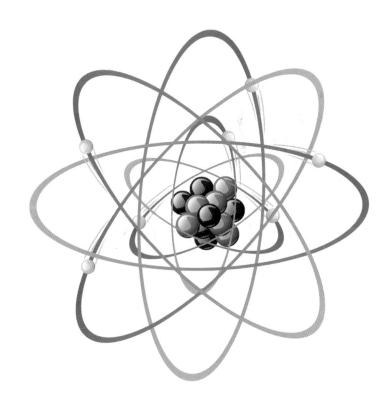

Emily Dodd

Author Emily Dodd
Consultant Fulbridge Academy

DK LONDON
Senior editor Lizzie Davey
Senior designer Jim Green
Additional editing Satu Fox, David Summers,
Megan Weal, Amina Youssef
Additional design Joanne Clark, Katie Knutton
Managing editor Laura Gilbert
Managing art editor Diane Peyton Jones
Pre-production producer Dragana Puvacic
Producer Basia Ossowska
Jacket editor Francesca Young
Art director Martin Wilson
Publishing director Sarah Larter

DK DELHI
Senior editor Vineetha Mokkil
Project editor Ishani Nandi
Assistant editors Shalini Agrawal, Shambhavi Thatte
Project art editor Nehal Verma
Art editor Shipra Jain
Assistant art editor Seepiya Sahni
Illustration designer Mohd Zishan
Managing editor Alka Thakur Hazarika
Managing art editor Romi Chakraborty
DTP designers Neeraj Bhatia, Bimlesh Tiwari
CTS manager Balwant Singh
Production manager Pankaj Sharma
Picture researcher Sakshi Saluja
Jacket designers Dheeraj Arora, Suzena Sengupta

First published in Great Britain in 2018 by
Dorling Kindersley Limited
80 Strand, London, WC2R 0RL

A CIP catalogue record for this book
is available from the British Library.
ISBN: 978-0-2413-1869-0

Printed and bound in China

A WORLD OF IDEAS:
SEE ALL THERE IS TO KNOW

www.dk.com

Contents

Find out why my fur is so soft on page 25.

The material world

Energy

Forces and movement

Our planet

Discover what makes lemon juice taste sour on page 71.

What is science?

Science helps us to answer questions. If we look for evidence and do experiments to test new ideas, we can understand how and why things work. We divide science into three main areas: chemistry, biology, and physics.

Science has helped invent every new technology, from the wheel to the iPad.

Living things

Biology is the study of living things and their surroundings. It includes how humans, plants, and animals behave, grow, and adapt to changes in their environment.

Movement and forces

Physics is the study of gravity, magnets, light, electricity, waves, sound, heat, energy, forces, and how objects move.

Why is science useful?

Expanding knowledge

When scientists investigate ideas and do experiments, they discover new information about the world around them. People can use that information to come up with more new ideas.

Solving problems

When we know more about how things work, we can invent new things to help us. For example, if we understand motion we can design faster cars.

Materials

Chemistry is the study of what things are made from. It explores how tiny particles called atoms can be arranged and changed to make different materials.

? True or false ?

1. Chemistry is the study of living things.

2. New discoveries can be unpopular when scientists first make them.

See pages 132–133 for the answers

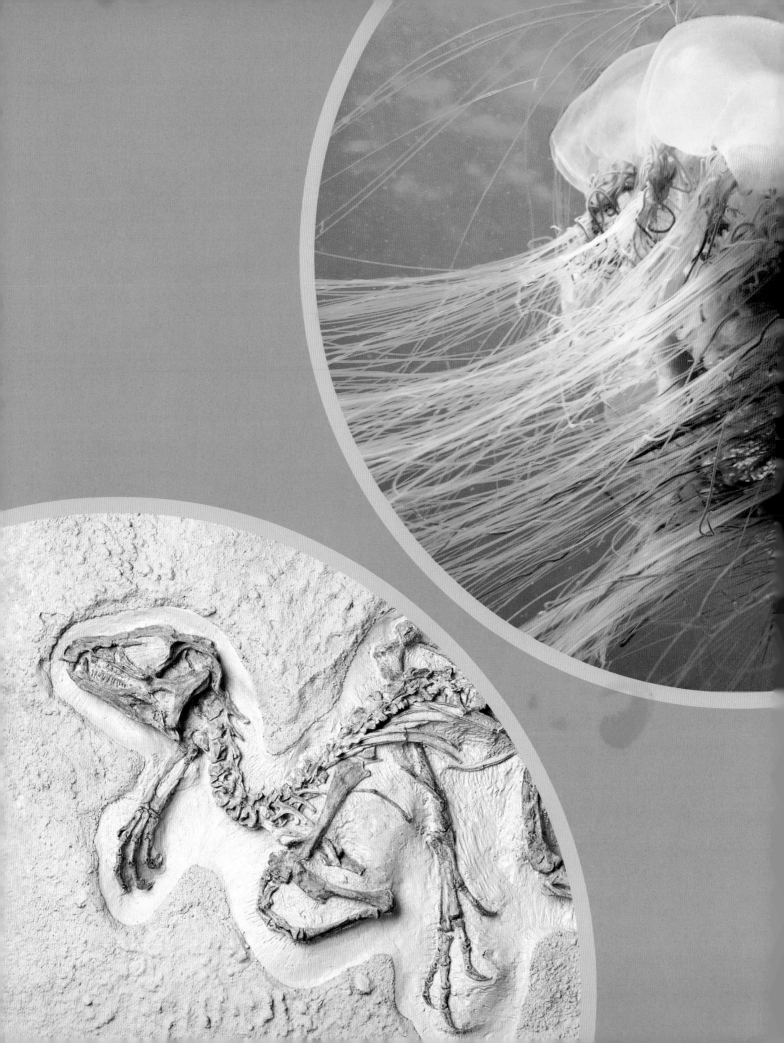

The Living World

Our world is bursting with life. From tiny bacteria to giant elephants, all living things need food and air to survive here on planet Earth.

What do living things need to survive?

All life on Earth needs a few basic things to survive. These are food, water, light, air, shelter, and a steady temperature. Occasionally, life can survive without one of these things, for example, in a dark cave.

Air

Living things take in gas from the air. They use it to turn food into energy. This is called respiration.

? True or false?

1. Giant tortoises are the animals that live longest.

2. Tardigrades can survive in space without any air.

3. Bristlecone pine trees can live for up to 5,000 years.

See pages 132–133 for the answers

Water

Animals and plants are mostly made from water and need water to stay alive. Animals have to find water to drink, while plants get it from the soil using their roots.

Sunlight

Heat and light from the Sun provide warmth. Most plants and animals need a constant temperature to survive.

Shelter

Animals need shelter to keep themselves and their young safe and at the right temperature. Shelter also allows them to hide from other animals.

Food

Living things need food to grow, move, and reproduce. Plants use sunlight to make their own food, and animals eat plants or other animals.

There are around 8.7 million different types of living things on Earth.

Which animals can survive in difficult environments?

Tardigrade

This microscopic animal can survive extreme temperatures. Tardigrades have been found living in the deep sea, the icy Antarctic, and even around volcanoes.

Anglerfish

The anglerfish survives at very low temperatures in the deep sea. Most animals would get crushed with so much water pushing down on them.

What is an animal?

Animals are living things that breathe, communicate, move, have babies, and can sense the world around them. They eat food to get energy. We sort animals into different groups depending on how similar they are to each other.

Amphibians

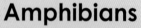

Amphibians include frogs, toads, and newts. They are cold-blooded as their body temperature is controlled by their environment. Most of them live part of their life in water and part on land.

Fish

Fish live in water and breathe oxygen by squirting water through gills on the sides of their bodies. Sharks are a type of fish.

Mammals

Mammals give birth to live young and feed them with milk. They have hair and are warm-blooded. Humans are mammals.

Invertebrates

Invertebrates are animals that don't have a backbone. A huge 97 per cent of animals are invertebrates, including insects, spider, crabs, and squishy things like snails.

Birds

Birds are the only animals with feathers, and most birds can fly. Birds lay eggs and have light bones. They have beaks and claws.

Reptiles

Reptiles are cold-blooded with dry, scaly skin and claws. They usually lay eggs. Some reptiles have shields or plates on their backs.

Are all living things animals?

Plants
Plants don't eat food. They make food from sunlight and carbon dioxide gas.

Fungi
Fungi include mushrooms, mould, and yeast. They are living things related to plants and animals.

? Picture quiz

What group does the jellyfish belong to?

See pages 132–133 for the answer

How big are bacteria?

All living things are made from tiny parts called cells. Bacteria are made from just one cell. They are the smallest living thing on Earth – so tiny that you can only see them with a microscope. Some bacteria are useful to us, while others make us sick.

Multiple shapes

Bacteria come in three shapes – rod-shaped, circular, or spiral. They reproduce by splitting themselves in half.

What other things are microscopic?

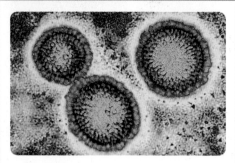

Viruses

Viruses are even smaller than bacteria. They live inside the cells of living things. When they reproduce they burst out of the cell, passing the virus on.

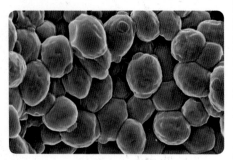

Fungi

Some fungi are microorganisms. Yeast is a single-celled fungus related to mushrooms. It eats sugar and releases gas. It is used in bread to make it rise.

Microorganisms

This photo of bacteria was taken using a microscope. Microscopic living things are called microorganisms.

How tiny is microscopic?

This yellow dot shows the size of a bacteria compared to the thickness of a human hair. Twenty bacteria could fit in a row across one hair.

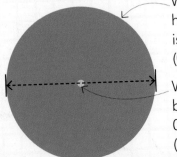

Width of human hair is 0.1 mm (0.003 in)

Width of bacteria is 0.005 mm (0.0001 in)

The width of a bacteria compared to the width of a human hair

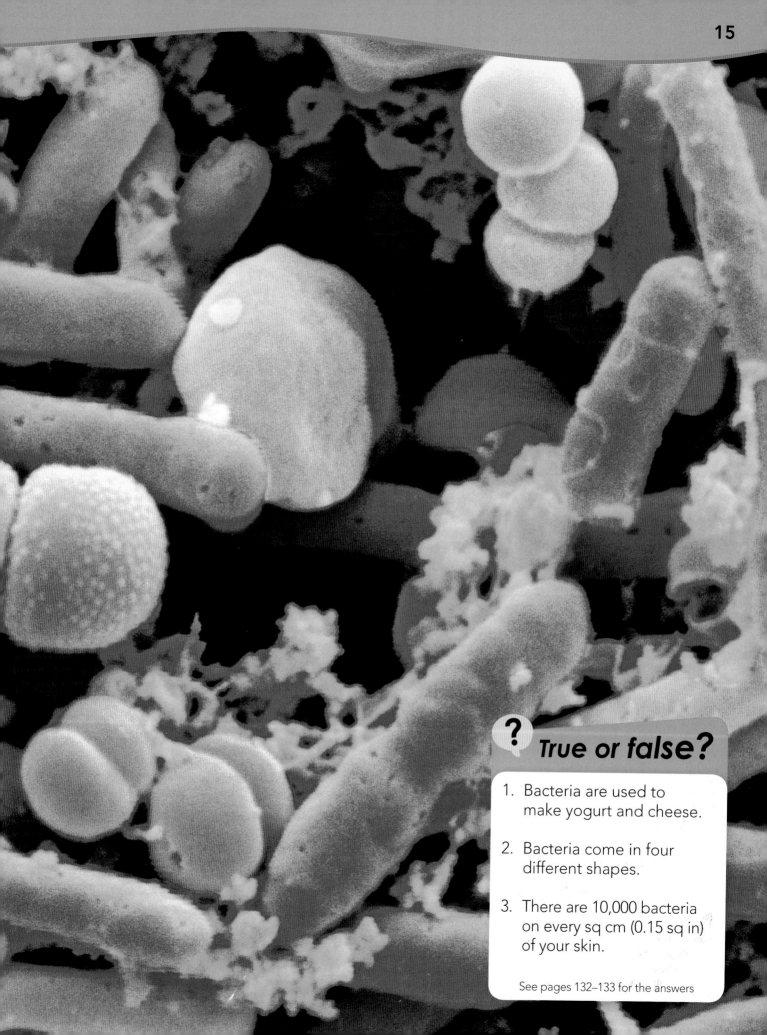

? True or false?

1. Bacteria are used to make yogurt and cheese.

2. Bacteria come in four different shapes.

3. There are 10,000 bacteria on every sq cm (0.15 sq in) of your skin.

See pages 132–133 for the answers

How do plants grow?

Plants begin as seeds. Seeds are little packets that contain everything a plant needs to grow, in the right conditions. Plants grow upwards and downwards, using energy from sunlight.

Shoot
The shoot grows upwards. There are two first leaves already on it.

Seed
The seed is protected by a shell called a coat. It breaks open when it's the right temperature and wet enough.

Root
The root breaks out and moves down to fix the plant in place. It takes water and food from the soil.

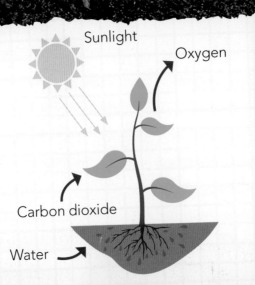

Photosynthesis
Plants take in sunlight, water, and a gas called carbon dioxide. They use these things to make a sugar called glucose. Glucose is food for the plant and gives it energy to grow. Once the light, water, and carbon dioxide are used up, the plant releases oxygen gas.

Sunlight

Oxygen

Carbon dioxide

Plant energy cycle   Water

A chemical called chlorophyll absorbs light energy from the Sun. It makes leaves look green.

True or f

1. Seeds can "sleep" for ... ars before starting to grow.

2. Most plants can grow without sunlight.

3. Dandelions spread their seeds in the wind.

See pages 132–133 for the answers

First leaves

The leaves open and take in sunlight to make food. The food gives the plant energy to grow.

Growing upwards

The stem brings water from the ground to the rest of the plant. It grows upwards using energy made by the leaves.

Roots

The plant's roots grow out and down. They help anchor the plant and supply it with water and other things it needs from the soil.

How can plants spread their seeds?

Exploding pods

Some plants grow their seeds in pods that burst open, sending seeds in all directions.

Wind

Some seeds are very light and shaped to float. They can spread to new locations on the wind.

Water

Many seeds float. They can travel down streams and along rivers to begin life in a new location. Coconuts float in the sea.

What makes things sticky?

Nature has many different ways to make things sticky. Sometimes things stick using hooks, suckers, or hairs. Other things stick using a sticky fluid or slime. Some plants produce fluids to catch insects that land on them.

Sticky ends

Tiny hair-like tentacles have blobs of sticky, sweet fluid on the end. Insects are attracted to the smell.

How else do things stick?

Burrs

Some plants spread their seeds by using hooks to attach themselves to an animal's fur. They fall off as the animal moves around.

Limpets

Limpets use a sticky fluid and a strong foot muscle to attach themselves to rocks. They twist and grind on the rock for a perfect fit.

Velcro

Velcro is a human-made material that has hooks on one side and loops on the other to stick and unstick things like shoes and coats. Unlike glue, which dries and hardens, it can be reused.

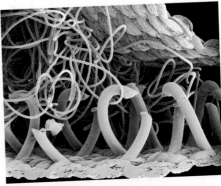

Hooks and loops

Pretend petals

The sticky leaves of the sundew plant are arranged to look like flower petals, which trick insects into visiting.

? True or false?

1. Some plants produce a sticky fluid to trap insects.

2. The glue on sticky notes was invented by accident.

3. Spiders' feet have lots of tiny sticky blobs on them to help them climb up walls.

See pages 132–133 for the answers

Are spiders insects?

A spider is different to an insect. It has eight legs instead of six and a body in two parts instead of an insect's three. Spiders are related to scorpions, ticks, and mites. Together, they form a group called the arachnids.

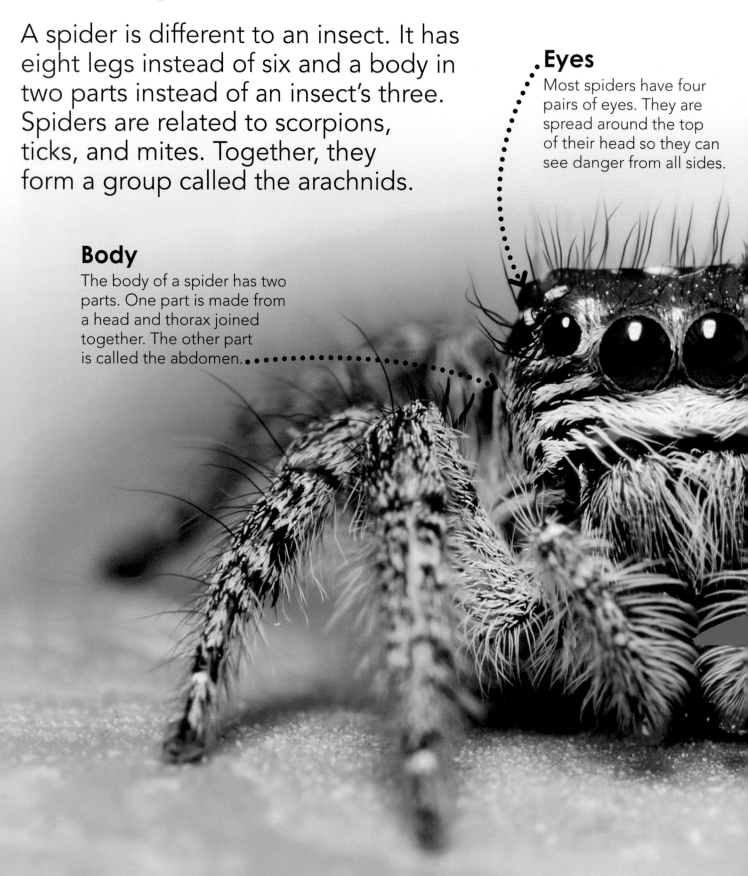

Eyes

Most spiders have four pairs of eyes. They are spread around the top of their head so they can see danger from all sides.

Body

The body of a spider has two parts. One part is made from a head and thorax joined together. The other part is called the abdomen.

Insect vs spider

The main differences between insects and spiders are body segments, legs, and wings.

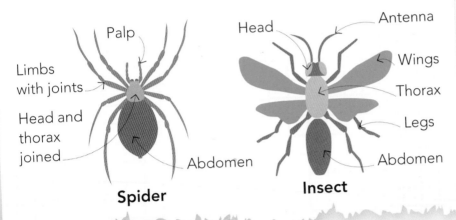

Spider — Palp, Limbs with joints, Head and thorax joined, Abdomen

Insect — Head, Antenna, Wings, Thorax, Legs, Abdomen

Legs

Spiders have eight jointed legs – four on each side. The hairs on their legs act like ears, picking up tiny movements in the air.

Why do spiders make silk?

To make egg cases

Female spiders make a silk bed and lay several hundred eggs in it. They wrap it in a silk ball and hang it somewhere safe.

To make webs

Spiders release silk to make sticky webs and nets to catch their food. They wrap trapped insects in silk and eat them later.

? True or false?

1. Some types of spiders have wings.

2. All spiders can make silk.

3. Spiders and insects both have a protective outer shell called an exoskeleton.

See pages 132–133 for the answers

What are feathers for?

Birds use feathers to keep warm, to hide, to scare off enemies, and even to show off! Feathers are light and strong. They join up to make a solid surface that helps birds fly.

Barbs

Feathers have tiny branches called barbs. Barbs hook together to make a smooth surface for flying. Birds use their beaks to move any hooks that are out of place.

Body feathers

Birds have soft, fluffy, short feathers called down on their bodies. These down feathers trap a layer of air, keeping the bird warm.

Why else do birds have feathers?

Camouflage

Many birds have feathers that blend in with their surroundings so they can hide from animals that eat them. This American bittern is brown like the marsh it lives in.

Display

Some male birds like the peacock show off their bright, colourful feathers to attract females. Others puff up their feathers to scare off enemies.

What are feathers made of?

Feathers are made of keratin, the same material fingernails and animal horns are made of. They have a strong tube in the middle called a quill. The soft part of the feather is called a vane.

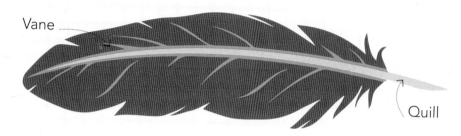

Vane

Quill

Flight feathers

Flight feathers are all slightly different shapes and lengths. Together, they make the wing the best possible shape for flying.

Picture quiz

The heaviest bird in the world cannot fly. What is it?

See pages 132–133 for the answer

Lift

As the wing feathers push air downwards, the air pushes back upwards lifting the bird in the air. Birds can also use air movements to help them lift and glide.

Tail feathers

Birds use their tail feathers to steer and balance themselves while flying. They also help the bird slow down for landing.

Which animals have fur?

Furry animals are called mammals. Mammals are a group of animals with fur, warm blood, and females that make milk to feed their young. Bears, bats, cats, and sheep are mammals. Humans are mammals too – the hair on our bodies is very thin fur!

Sharp teeth

Cheetahs are carnivores, which means they eat other animals. Sharp, pointed teeth help them to rip meat from the bone.

Dark spots

Each cheetah has its own pattern of spots – no two cheetahs have the same pattern.

Seasonal fur

Some mammals have fur that changes over time. In summer, arctic hares have thick, dark fur. In winter, they shed their dark fur and grow a thick, white coat. This helps them stay camouflaged all year round.

Dark summer coat blends in with rocks and plants.

White winter coat blends in with snow.

Sensitive whiskers

Many mammals have a stiff, long type of hair called whiskers. Sensors at the base of these hairs tell the animal if they are touching an object.

Camouflage

The sandy colour and spotted pattern on a cheetah's coat helps it stay hidden while hunting. This is called camouflage.

? True or false?

1. All mammals live on land.

2. Reptiles also have fur on their bodies.

3. Sea otters have the thickest fur of all animals.

See pages 132–133 for the answers

Do all animals have the same type of fur?

Hedgehog

Hedgehogs have stiff, sharp hairs called spines. They can roll into a spiky ball to protect themselves from danger.

Chinchilla

Chinchillas have incredibly soft fur because at least 60 hairs grow from each hair follicle. Humans have one to three hairs in each follicle.

Whales

Whales are born with a small amount of fur on their chin and upper jaw, a bit like a beard and moustache. They lose this fur shortly after they are born.

What do lions eat?

Lions choose from a range of animals that they can catch and eat. Hunters like lions are called predators. The animals they hunt are called their prey. Lions are at the top of the food chain because nothing hunts them.

Zebras have stripy coats so lions can't see their shape in long grass.

Food chain

A food chain shows where energy comes from. The lion gets energy from eating the zebra. The zebra gets energy from eating grass and the grass gets energy from the Sun. The lion needs the whole food chain to survive.

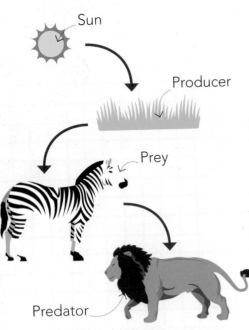

Sun

Producer

Prey

Predator

The lion is at the top of the food chain.

What makes lions good hunters?

Sharp teeth and rough tongues

Lions have sharp teeth to help them tear into their prey, and rough tongues covered in tiny spines to scrape meat from the bones.

Strong claws and paws

Sharp claws and strong paws help lions catch and hold prey. A lion's paw is the size of a dinner plate! Loose skin on their bellies protects them from the kicks of hoofed animals like zebras.

On the run

Lions mostly eat animals their own size or bigger. They prefer young, old, or injured animals that are easier to catch.

Chasing prey

Lions hunt in packs, with lionesses doing most of the hunting. One chases the prey towards a group of other lions.

? True or false?

1. Male lions do most of the hunting.

2. Lions spend 18–20 hours a day sleeping.

3. Wild lions live in Australia.

See pages 132–133 for the answers

How do butterflies grow?

Butterflies go through an amazing transformation from wiggly worm-like caterpillars to elegant, colourful flying insects. This life-changing process is called metamorphosis.

Eggs

Female butterflies lay tiny eggs that they stick onto leaves. The eggs are different shapes depending on the type of butterfly that laid them.

Frog life cycle

Butterflies aren't the only animals that go through the process of metamorphosis. Frogs change from eggs called frogspawn to fish-like tadpoles, then grow legs, arms, and lose their tails to become frogs.

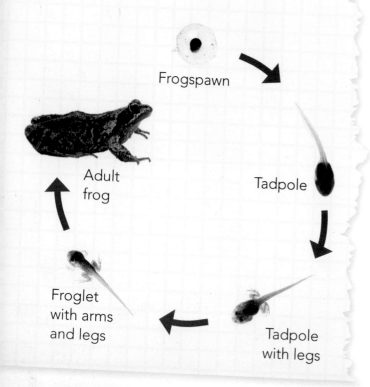

Frogspawn

Tadpole

Tadpole with legs

Froglet with arms and legs

Adult frog

Breaking out

The new butterfly breaks out of the chrysalis. Its wings are soft and damp. They must stretch and dry out before the butterfly can fly.

Caterpillar

Caterpillars hatch from eggs. They eat the leaf their egg was stuck to first. Then they eat more leaves from the same type of plant. They need to eat lots of leaves to grow bigger.

Chrysalis

When caterpillars are fully grown, they stick to a leaf or twig and form a hard layer of skin around themselves, called a chrysalis. The caterpillar changes inside the chrysalis.

Adult

Adult butterflies have beautiful colours and are able to fly. Male and female adults mate to make new eggs.

Do butterflies have special features?

Tongue
Butterflies have long, straw-like tongues. They use them to sip a sugary liquid called nectar from flowers.

Wing "eyes"
Some butterflies have eye-like spots on their wings. The markings trick animals that might want to eat the butterfly into attacking its wings instead of the body.

? True or false?

1. Caterpillars grow bigger by shedding their skin.

2. Chrysalises are usually coloured green or brown to blend in with surrounding plants.

3. Butterflies can taste with their feet.

See pages 132–133 for the answers

Why don't polar bears freeze?

Adaptions are things that make animals well suited to the place where they live. Polar bears have adapted to live in the freezing cold of the Arctic.

Eyes
A clear extra eyelid closes so the polar bear can see underwater. The eyelid also works in a snowstorm.

Nose
Polar bears have an amazing sense of smell to help them to find food. They can sniff out a seal over 30 km (18.5 miles) away!

Charles Darwin
Charles Darwin realized that over millions of years animals gradually change to become better suited to their environments. These changes are called evolution.

Charles Darwin

Hollow hairs
Each polar bear hair is a clear, hollow tube. The Sun's light travels through the hair to the bear's black skin, which absorbs heat.

Fat
Up to 10 cm (4 in) of fat lies under the skin, to keep the bear warm.

Fur
A thick, shorter layer of fur traps air to keep the polar bear warm. Longer hairs stick together to form a waterproof layer in water.

Paws
Huge paws work like snowshoes on the slippery ice. They are also slightly webbed for swimming.

Polar bears can swim 100 km (60 miles) without a rest.

Which ice age animals became extinct?

Irish elk
When the snow melted, the Irish elk may have got its giant antlers stuck in bushes, making it easy for other animals to hunt.

Woolly mammoth
When it got warmer, more humans hunted mammoths. Eventually there were none left. This is called extinction.

? True or false?

1. A polar bear's favourite food is penguins.

2. Ice age bears were even bigger than polar bears.

3. Polar bears live in the Antarctic.

See pages 132–133 for the answers

Buried treasure

Scientists called palaeontologists find fossils and piece them together like jigsaws. They can work out what dinosaurs were like and how they behaved.

How do we know dinosaurs existed?

Occasionally, after dinosaurs died, they were buried and squashed. Their bones eventually turned into rocks called fossils. There are also fossils of horns, shells, plants, poos, footprints, and even sand-ripple marks on seashores.

? Quick quiz

1. Why are fossils very rare?

2. Can insects trapped in tree sap become fossils?

3. What is the name palaeontologists use for fossilized dinosaur poo?

See pages 132–133 for the answers

How are fossils made?

Fossils are made when a dead dinosaur is quickly buried and the hard parts are replaced by minerals to become rock. We find fossils in the ground millions of years after the dinosaur lived on Earth.

Dinosaur dies

A dinosaur dies and is quickly buried by sand, ash, or mud.

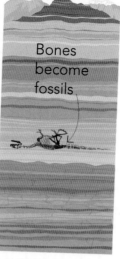

Bones become fossils

Layers squash the buried dinosaur, and the hard parts get replaced by minerals.

Fossils discovered

The rock lifts up and gets worn away over time and the fossils are uncovered.

Bone into rock

The hard parts of this dinosaur have changed into rock. Minerals and chemicals have slowly replaced the bones.

Prehistoric animals

Dinosaurs became extinct 65 million years ago but we know lots about them from clues left behind in their fossils.

What else did dinosaurs leave behind?

Footprints

Some dinosaur footprints got buried under layers of sand, ash, or mud. They were fossilized in the same way as bones.

Coprolites

Fossilized dinosaur poos are called coprolites. They can tell palaeontologists what dinosaurs ate.

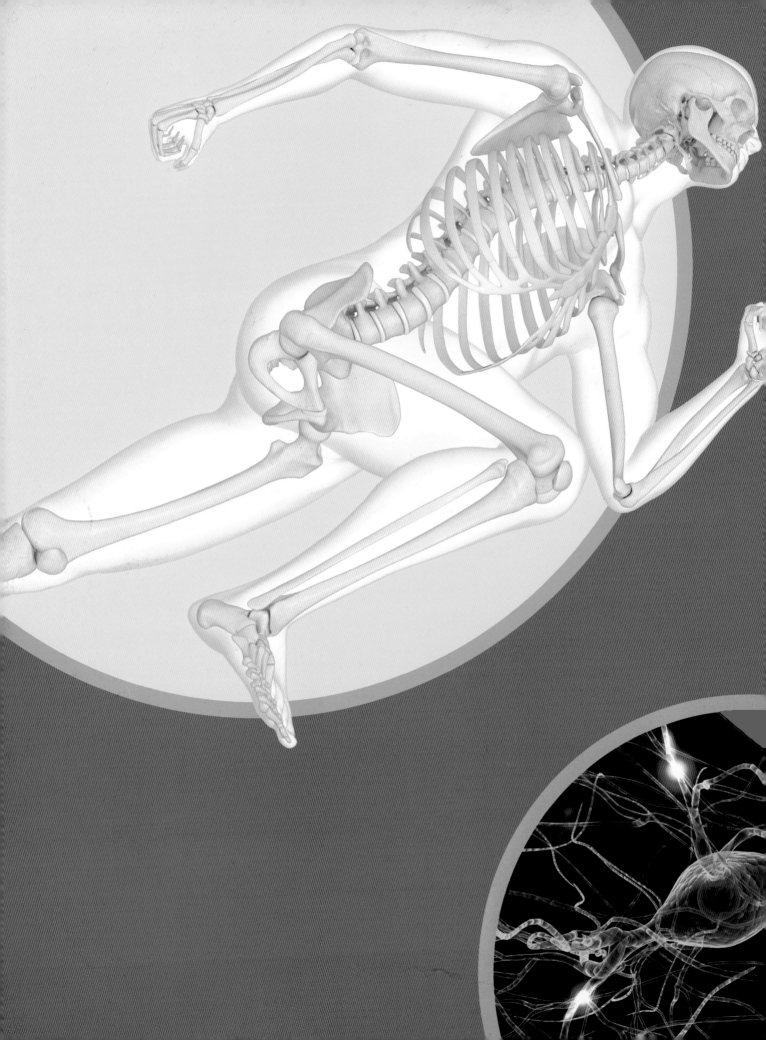

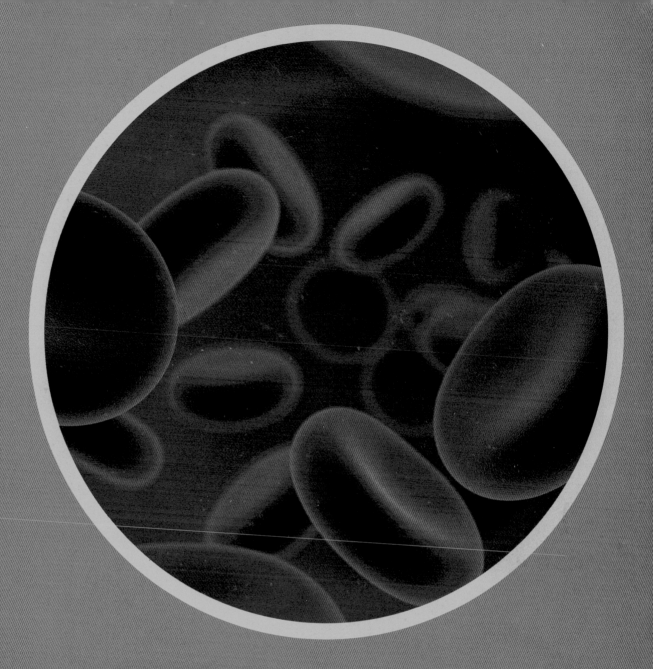

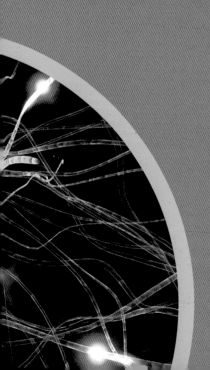

Human Body

Our bodies are made up of cells, organs, and systems. All these parts have important jobs to do to keep us living and moving.

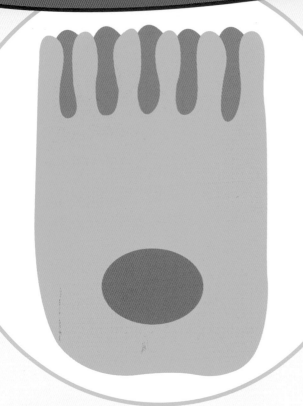

Cells

Each type of cell is a different shape and size depending on the job it does. The intestines contain frilly cells that absorb nutrients from food.

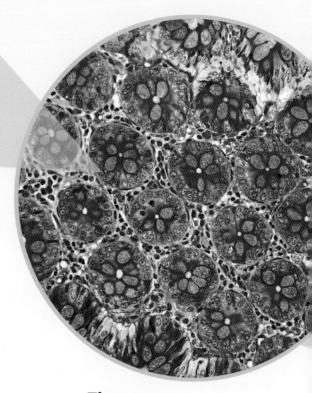

Tissues

Cells join together to make different types of tissue. The intestines are made up of four types of tissue. These include muscles that push your food through the intestines.

What is my body made of?

Everything in the body is made from tiny parts called cells. Lots of cells joined together make a tissue. Tissues work together as organs. Organs join together in systems. Everything has a job to do to keep the body working.

What jobs can cells do?

Carry signals

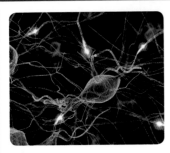

Nerve or neuron cells have lots of branches. Nerve cells connect together to carry electrical signals to the brain from all over the body.

Move things

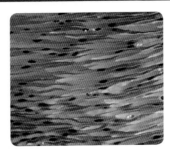

Muscle cells use energy to tighten and become shorter. When they relax they go back to being long again. This lets them pull body parts around, such as your arms and legs.

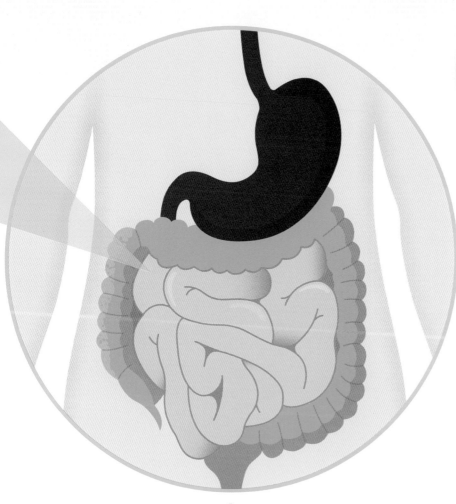

Stem cells can turn into skin, muscle, or blood depending on what your body needs.

Organ systems

Organs work together in groups called systems. The intestines are part of the digestive system. This system includes the organs that process food.

? Quick quiz

1. Which body cells are round and doughnut-shaped to carry oxygen?

2. Which body system processes food?

3. What is the heaviest organ in the body?

See pages 132–133 for the answers

How big is my skin?

The skin is the waterproof outer layer of the body. It protects our body from sunshine, keeps germs out, and keeps us at the right temperature. The skin is the heaviest of the body's organs.

Skin layers

Our skin has two main layers. The top layer is called the epidermis. The layer below, which hairs grow from, is called the dermis. Fat under the skin cushions us from knocks and bangs.

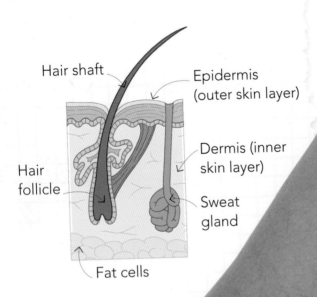

Hair shaft

Epidermis (outer skin layer)

Dermis (inner skin layer)

Hair follicle

Sweat gland

Fat cells

Skin colour

The skin's colour is created by a chemical called melanin. The more melanin you have in your skin, the darker it will be.

Fingerprint

Every single person in the world has a unique swirly skin pattern on their fingertips. This is called a fingerprint.

Keratin

Skin is made of tiny parts called cells. These cells are made from a tough material called keratin.

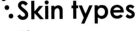

More than 10 million dead skin cells flake off our bodies every day!

Skin types

Skin on some parts of the body is different than on others. The skin on our hands is tougher and thicker than the skin on our face.

What else is made of keratin?

Hair

Hair grows from holes called follicles in the skin's dermis layer. It grows everywhere on the body except the palms of our hands, soles of our feet, and lips.

Nails

Hard nails protect the ends of our fingers and toes. They also help our fingers to pick up objects or open things.

? True or false?

1. The thinnest skin is found on the eyelids.

2. Skin is waterproof.

3. Skin becomes less elastic with age, making it look wrinkly and saggy.

See pages 132–133 for the answers

What do bones do?

The human body contains 206 bones that form a skeleton. Some bones move, such as our legs when we walk. Other parts of the skeleton are there to protect our inner body parts and to support our body.

Inside a bone

The outer layer is made of strong compact bone. Beneath is spongy bone that contains bone marrow. Bone marrow supplies blood cells to the body.

Bone marrow

Blood vessels

Spongy bone

Compact bone

Cross-section of a bone

Pelvis

The pelvis is a circle of bones that include the hipbones. It protects the organs that are lower down in the body.

Femur

This is the strongest, heaviest, and longest bone in the body. The ball-shaped top allows the leg to rotate at the hip.

How do we see bones?

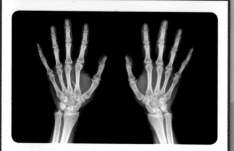

X-rays

Doctors shine waves of energy called X-rays through our bodies. X-rays bounce off our bones to show us what they look like.

Spongy bones

The head of the bone is mostly made of spongy bone. This type of bone has lots of little holes inside it that make it lighter.

Skull

The skull contains 22 bones that are locked together to protect the brain. The lower jaw is the only bone in the skull that moves.

Spine

The spine keeps us upright. It allows movement and protects the nerves that carry signals between the brain and the body.

Ribcage

This cage of bones protects the soft lungs and heart. It moves up and down to help inflate the lungs as we breathe.

Bendy joints

Joints are areas where bones join together. Joints allow us to bend or rotate parts of our body.

? Quick quiz

1. How many bones does the skull contain?

2. What part of the body contains the most bones?

3. How many joints are there in a skeleton?

See pages 132–133 for the answers

How do people move?

Muscles work together to make the different parts of our body move. Muscles only pull, they can't push. One muscle pulls a body part one way and another pulls it the other way. Muscles work in groups so we can move in all directions.

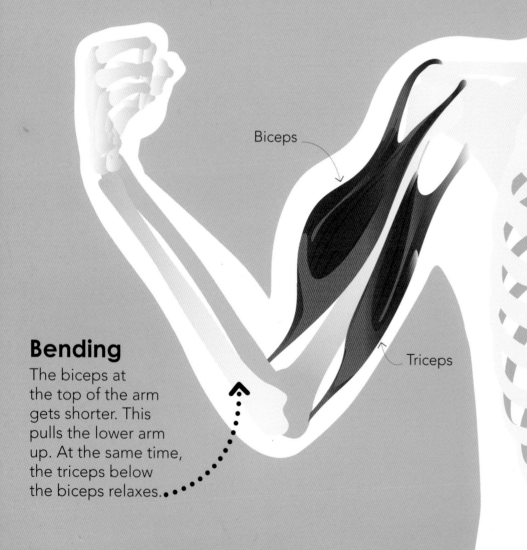

Biceps

Triceps

Bending

The biceps at the top of the arm gets shorter. This pulls the lower arm up. At the same time, the triceps below the biceps relaxes.

What happens when a person exercises?

Stronger muscles

The body makes new muscle fibres after exercise. This means muscles get bigger and stronger the more you use them!

Longer and stronger

If you exercise regularly, you'll be able to do it for longer. Heart and breathing muscles get stronger when you use them more. Running, swimming, and cycling all exercise the heart and lungs.

Working together

Muscles work with joints to move the body around. Muscles are connected to the bones by tissues called tendons.

True or false?

1. The biggest muscle in our body is in our bottom.

2. You use 300 different muscles just to stand up without falling over.

3. Muscles can push or pull.

See pages 132–133 for the answers

Biceps

Joints

Joints are the places where one bone joins another to allow you to move. Joints have fluid in them to help make movement smooth.

Straightening

The triceps under the arm gets shorter, which pulls the lower arm down. At the same time, the biceps above it relaxes and the arm straightens.

Triceps

How do I breathe?

Muscles pull air in and out of our lungs when we breathe. Air enters the body through the nose and mouth. It travels down the windpipe and into the lungs. We need to breathe to stay alive.

Inside our lungs

The lungs are big, spongy bags full of tubes that end in air sacks called alveoli. Alveoli transfer oxygen gas into the blood.

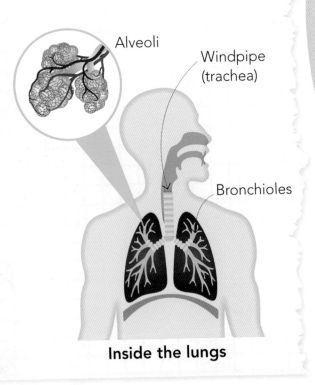

Alveoli

Windpipe
(trachea)

Bronchioles

Inside the lungs

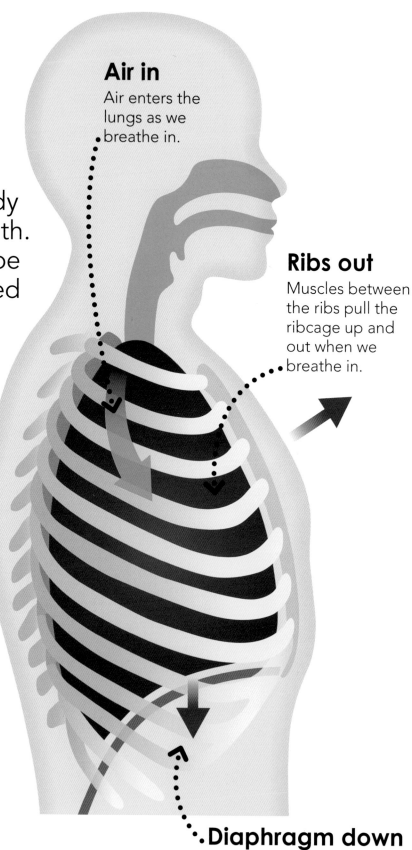

Air in
Air enters the lungs as we breathe in.

Ribs out
Muscles between the ribs pull the ribcage up and out when we breathe in.

Diaphragm down
The diaphragm is a sheet of muscle that pulls down to inflate the lungs.

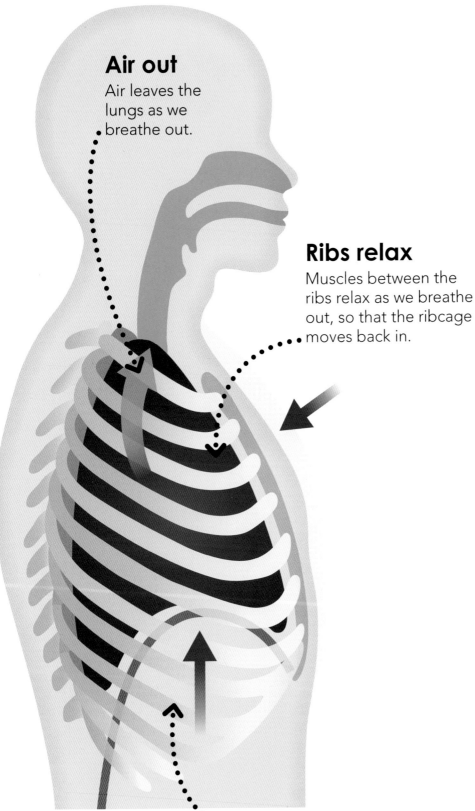

Air out
Air leaves the lungs as we breathe out.

Ribs relax
Muscles between the ribs relax as we breathe out, so that the ribcage moves back in.

Diaphragm up
The diaphragm relaxes to push air up and out of the lungs.

How do animals breathe under water?

Blowholes
Whales and dolphins hold their breath underwater. They must get to the surface of the water, where they breathe using a "blowhole" on the head.

Gills
Fish, like this shark, suck water into their mouth and push it through organs called gills that take the oxygen they need from the water.

? Quick quiz

1. Where does the oxygen we need come from?

2. How many breaths do we take a day?

3. What is another name for the windpipe?

See pages 132–133 for the answers

What makes my blood move?

The heart is a muscle about the size of a fist. It's a pump that squashes in and out around 80 times every minute, moving blood all around the body. If the heart stops pumping, the body stops working immediately.

Blood flow

Blood moves around the body in a circuit. It travels to the lungs to collect oxygen gas and delivers the oxygen around the body before coming back to the heart.

What do blood cells do?

Carry gases

Red blood cells carry oxygen and release it around the body. They also carry waste gas called carbon dioxide.

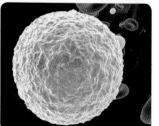

Fight germs

White blood cells kill germs by squirting killer chemicals at them or by changing shape and swallowing them up.

Vein

Blood travelling back to the heart from the body no longer carries oxygen. It travels through tubes called veins.

Blood carrying oxygen to the body

It takes just 20 seconds for blood to make a complete journey around the body.

Blood without oxygen travels to the lungs

Circulatory system

The heart and tubes that connect the blood to the body are called the circulatory system. Blood carries water, gases, sugar, and heat.

Capillaries are tubes that connect up the veins and the arteries.

The heart pumps blood around the circulatory system.

Blood travelling through arteries carries oxygen.

Blood travelling in veins has delivered its oxygen.

Artery

Blood being pumped from the heart to the body via the lungs carries oxygen in tubes called arteries.

Valve

Little doors in the heart called valves only open one way so that the blood can only travel in one direction.

Heart muscle

The heart is made of cardiac muscle tissue, a special tissue that is only found in the heart.

Key

 With oxygen

 Without oxygen

? True or false?

1. Blood is as salty as sea water.

2. Blood cells are made inside the lungs.

3. Blood that travels to the lungs doesn't contain oxygen.

See pages 132–133 for the answers

Where does my food go?

The food we eat goes on a journey through our bodies. It travels down a tube in the throat called the oesophagus and into the stomach, where acid breaks it down. Next, it moves through the intestines. Then, finally, solid food waste is pushed out as poo.

Mouth

We first break our food down by chewing it with our teeth, moving it around with our tongue, and mixing it with saliva.

Oesophagus

When we swallow, the food travels down a tube called the oesophagus and into our stomach.

Stomach

The stomach is a soft bag that adds liquid chemicals to food to break it down into tiny pieces. It churns the food around to make a soupy liquid.

? Quick quiz

1. How do the intestines move food along?

2. What foods give our body a quick release of energy, but can be bad for us if we eat too much of them?

3. How long does it take for food to pass all the way through our bodies?

See pages 132–133 for the answers

Inside the small intestine

The walls of the small intestines have lots of wiggly folds. These increase the area that is able to absorb (take in) food. Tiny hair-like villi absorb the goodness from the food and transfer it to the blood.

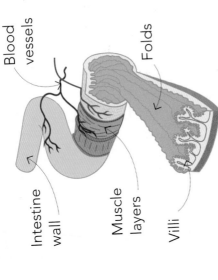

Blood vessels

Folds

Intestine wall

Muscle layers

Villi

Cutaway of the small intestine

Small intestine

The mushed-up food and liquid travels through the small intestine. Goodness from the food travels through the walls of the intestine and into our blood.

Large intestine

Waste food that we don't need goes into the large intestine. It stays there until we push it out as poo.

How does food help our bodies?

Proteins

Proteins are found in meat, fish, beans, nuts, and eggs. They help our bodies to grow and to repair.

Carbohydrates

Carbohydrates are found in pasta, potatoes, rice, and bread. They give our bodies the energy that they need.

Fruits and vegetables

Fruits and vegetables contain fibre that helps us digest food. They also contain vitamins and minerals that keep our body parts working.

What controls my body?

The brain is the control centre for the body. It is connected to the senses by a network of tiny paths called nerves. Signals for things such as hunger and thirst also travel along nerves. Every time we move, breathe, or think, our brains are at work.

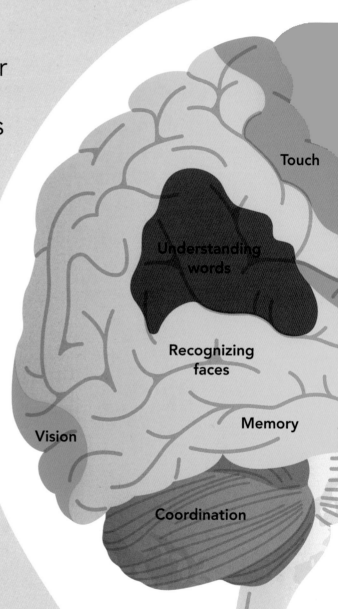

Touch

Understanding words

Recognizing faces

Memory

Vision

Coordination

How is the brain connected to the body?

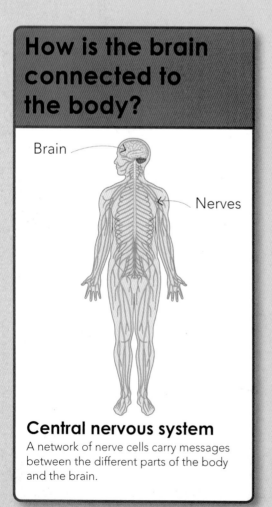

Brain

Nerves

Central nervous system

A network of nerve cells carry messages between the different parts of the body and the brain.

Brain stem

Signals from the senses and signals that tell the body to move travel through the brain stem.

Different jobs

Different parts of the brain are responsible for different jobs in the body. Signals travel between these areas and all the parts of the body.

Planning

Thinking

Judging

Speaking

Feeling

aring

Taste

Smell

eelings

Nerve cells

Thoughts travel as electrical signals along dendrites to the nerve ending. Chemicals pass the thought on to the next nerve.

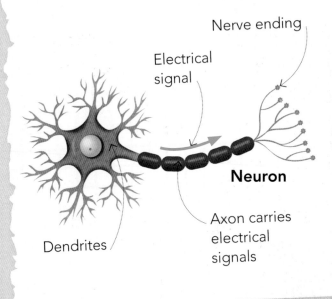

Nerve ending

Electrical signal

Neuron

Dendrites

Axon carries electrical signals

Brain hemispheres

The two sides of the brain are called hemispheres. The right hemisphere controls the left side of the body and the left hemisphere controls the right.

Key

- Senses
- Thoughts
- Language
- Movement
- Understanding the world
- Feelings
- Coordination

? Quick quiz

1. What happens in the brain during sleep?

2. How many hemispheres does the brain have?

3. How did the ancient Egyptians remove the brain when they were making a mummy?

See pages 132–133 for the answers

How do cuts heal?

When we get a cut, blood comes out of the break in our skin and repairs the damage. It sticks together and changes from a liquid to a solid called a clot. A hard scab forms on top and new skin cells are made underneath. When the wound has healed, the scab falls off.

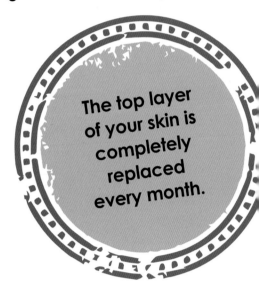

The top layer of your skin is completely replaced every month.

Cuts and scrapes

When you get a cut, blood leaks out and starts to clot. A clot is solid blood that seals a wound. Three types of blood cell work together to heal the cut.

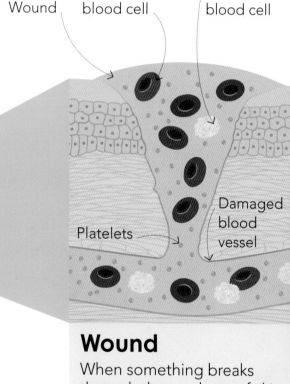

Wound

Red blood cell

White blood cell

Platelets

Damaged blood vessel

Wound

When something breaks through the top layer of skin into a blood vessel, blood leaks out. White blood cells fight germs by squirting killer chemicals at them and swallowing them.

How do bones mend?

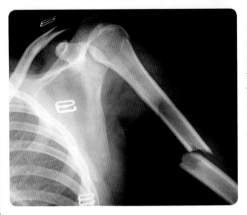

Healing fractures

If a bone breaks it can heal itself, if it is kept still. Blood fills the gap with a clot, which then turns into a body tissue called cartilage. Finally, new bone is created by the body's cells.

? True or false?

1. The top layer of your skin is replaced every year.

2. Leeches can stop blood from clotting.

3. A group of tiny cuts is called a blister.

See pages 132–133 for the answers

Red blood cells and fibrin form a mesh.

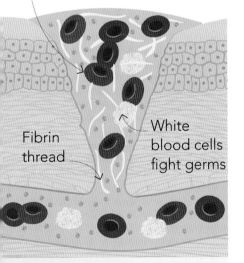

Fibrin thread

White blood cells fight germs

Blood clot helps close up the wound.

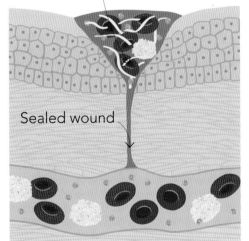

Sealed wound

Hard scab

Tissue starts to repair.

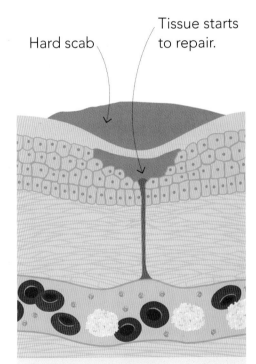

Closing up

Cells called platelets change shape and make strands called fibrin. These strands act like a net to trap red blood cells and gather them together.

Clot

When enough red blood cells are trapped by the fibrin net, they make a clot. Liquid blood can turn into solid blood in just a few minutes.

Healed skin

A hard layer called a scab forms at the top of the clot. New skin cells are made under the clot. The scab falls off after a few days, leaving new skin.

How does my body fight sickness?

Germs can enter our bodies and make us sick. The body has a system in place to stop germs getting into the body and to fight those that do get in.

Ears

Ears produce a yellowish, waxy fluid that fights germs by pushing them out.

Skin

The skin is a waterproof layer that covers and protects the inner parts of our body, keeping germs on the outside.

White blood cells

White blood cells kill germs in the body. They travel around in the blood. When they find germs, the white blood cells squirt killer chemicals at them or swallow them up.

1. White blood cell captures germs.

2. White blood cell surrounds germs.

3. Waste is expelled.

Some white blood cells surround germs and then destroy them

Intestines

Mucus in the intestines catches germs and stops them getting into the blood. Friendly bacteria help food digestion and stop germs growing.

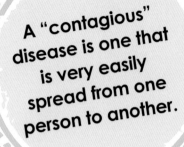

A "contagious" disease is one that is very easily spread from one person to another.

Eyes

Eyes produce tears that wash away germs. A chemical in tears can make germs explode!

What else helps us fight sicknesses?

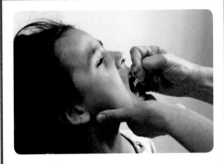

Vaccines

Vaccines give our body a tiny amount of a disease, so our bodies can learn how to fight it off.

Medicine

Medicines are used to cure sickness or make us feel better. They come in many different forms.

Lungs

A sticky substance called mucus traps any germs we breathe into our lungs. Hairs push mucus and germs up our throats and we swallow them into our stomachs.

Stomach acid

The stomach contains a strong chemical called hydrochloric acid. This acid kills many of the germs we swallow.

? Quick quiz

1. Which types of blood cells fight germs?

2. What do tonsils do for the body?

3. How does saliva (spit) protect our body?

See pages 132–133 for the answers

The Material World

Materials can change shape and be used to make things. They can be mixed together and separated or they can react together to make new things.

What is everything made of?

From the smallest insects to massive stars, everything in the Universe is built from tiny particles called atoms. Atoms are so small we can't even see them. They contain even smaller particles called protons, neutrons, and electrons.

What happens when you split an atom?

Nuclear energy

Splitting atoms releases large amounts of energy. This can be used to create electricity in a nuclear power station.

Nuclear explosion

When atoms split, neutrons ping into other atoms, making them split too. This can create a huge explosion of heat and energy.

Particle accelerator

Scientists speed atomic particles along tracks and crash them into each other in order to learn more about atoms.

Electrons

Electrons are negatively charged particles that move around. They are attracted to the atom by protons.

Nucleus

The nucleus is at the centre of the atom. It is made up of protons and neutrons.

Molecules

Atoms stick together in groups called molecules. The shells of atoms overlap and they share electrons between them. For example, water is made from two hydrogen atoms and one oxygen atom.

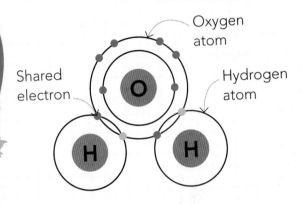

Oxygen atom

Shared electron

Hydrogen atom

Structure of a water molecule

Protons

Protons are positively charged particles. They attract electrons to the atom. The number of protons in an atom is called the atomic number.

Neutrons

Neutrons are particles that have no electric charge. All atoms have equal numbers of neutrons and protons, apart from hydrogen, which has one proton and no neutrons.

? Quick quiz

1. Which atomic particle has no charge?

2. What do we call electricity made by the heat released by splitting atoms?

3. What do we call atoms that are joined together in a group?

See pages 132–133 for the answers

Why does chocolate melt?

Materials can be solid, liquid, or gas, depending on the temperature and how squashed they are. Chocolate is solid at room temperature. When we heat it up, the tiny particles inside the chocolate start to move past each other. This makes the chocolate melt and change into a liquid.

Solid

A solid keeps its shape. If you stack solids they make a pile not a pool.

? Quick quiz

1. What do we call the process of changing from a liquid to a solid?

2. Which state of matter has the most tightly packed particles?

3. What metal is liquid at room temperature?

See pages 132–133 for the answers

> Water is the only substance found naturally in all three forms on Earth – solid, liquid, and gas.

What melts in nature?

Glaciers

Big sheets of ice, known as glaciers, start to melt as the temperature increases. Sometimes huge chunks of ice fall into the sea as a result.

Volcanoes

Rock melts when it is very hot and lots of weight pushes down on it. This hot, melted rock explodes out of volcanoes as lava.

Changing states

Materials can sometimes change from being solid to liquid, and then to gas. This happens if we add heat or squash them. Materials can then change back as they cool or if we stop squashing them.

Solids have particles packed close together and in straight lines.

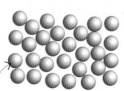

Liquids have particles in small groups that move past each other.

Gases have particles that move away from each other in all directions.

Liquid

A liquid can be poured. It makes a pool not a pile.

How can I get salt out of saltwater?

Saltwater is a mixture of water and salt. The salt has dissolved into the water so we can no longer see the individual grains. We can get salt out of saltwater by letting the water evaporate, or through a process called distillation.

Salty flat

Salt flats are shallow pools of saltwater that are covered by a crust of salt.

Salt deposits

Warmth from the Sun makes the water evaporate (turn into gas). The solid salt does not evaporate and is left behind.

The world's largest salt flat contains 11 billion tonnes (12 billion tons) of salt.

What is distillation?

Distillation is when liquid is separated from a mixture. Boiling saltwater turns the water into a gas called water vapour. The gas goes into a tube, cools, and turns back into liquid. The water drips into a container and salt is left behind.

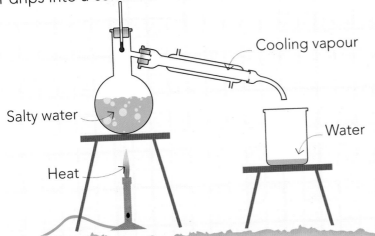

Cooling vapour

Salty water

Water

Heat

Mining for minerals

People collect the salt by raking it up into piles. These are transported to factories to be turned into the salt we eat.

How else can mixtures be separated?

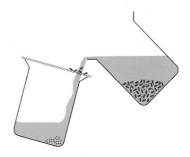

Sieving

A sieve collects larger solids but allows smaller solids through. For example, it could separate pebbles from sand.

Filtering

A filter is a material that works like a net to trap solid materials and let only liquids through.

? Quick quiz

1. Can you drink saltwater?

2. Is the water in rivers and lakes salty?

3. What is it called when a liquid is warmed up and turns into a gas?

See pages 132–133 for the answers

What is a metal?

Metals are useful materials. They can be used for making different things depending on how they behave. They can be strong, shiny, or malleable, which means they can be shaped easily. Metals also let electricity move through them.

Mercury is the only metal that is a liquid at room temperature.

Malleable (easily shaped)

Aluminium

Aluminium is a light, strong metal that does not rust easily. It can be shaped into lots of different things, such as bicycles, drinks cans, and planes.

Iron

Iron is hard, strong, and long-lasting. When iron is left in the open air for too long, it rusts, and so is often coated in paint to protect against this.

Hard and strong

What do we get by mixing two metals?

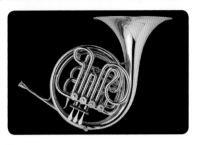

Brass
A mix of two or more metals is called an alloy. Brass is a mixture of copper and zinc. It is used to make musical instruments and coins.

Steel
Steel is iron with other things added to make it less likely to rust, or to make it stronger. It is used to make cutlery, ships, and tools.

? Picture quiz

What happens when iron is left exposed to the air?

See pages 132–133 for the answer

Copper
Copper can be easily shaped into wire or flattened into sheets. Copper is a good conductor, which means electricity passes through it easily.

Conducts electricity and heat

Gold
Gold is a shiny, beautiful soft metal. It can be easily melted and shaped. Gold is rare and expensive.

Shiny

Extracting oil

Engineers drill into the ground to find oil. They pump water down the hole to where the oil is. Oil floats on water, so it rises up and comes out of the ground.

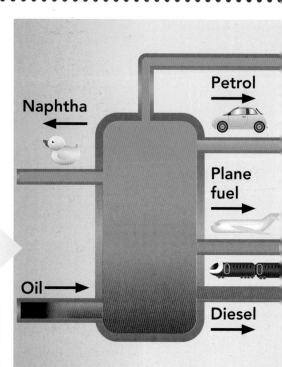

Petrol

Naphtha

Plane fuel

Oil

Diesel

Refining oil

Oil is made from various liquids that all boil at different temperatures. When it is heated up, the oil separates into different things, such as petrol and naphtha. Naphtha is used to make plastic.

How is plastic made?

Most plastics are made from crude oil. Crude oil was made when tiny plants and animals called plankton got squashed underground, millions of years ago. It takes many steps to turn oil into plastic.

What can plastic be used for?

Carrier bags

Plastic is used for carrier bags, because they need to be light and strong. Plastic bags should be re-used because they take a long time to break down if you throw them away.

Toys

Plastic toys come in bright colours, and will last a long time even if you play with them a lot. Plastic can easily be turned into different shapes to create any toy the inventors come up with.

? True or false?

1. Plastic is made from oil.

2. 80 per cent of our plastic worldwide is recycled.

3. It takes around 500 years for a plastic bottle to decompose.

See pages 132–133 for the answers

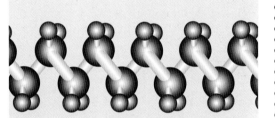

Chemical process

Naphtha is heated and chemicals are added. This makes the tiny particles it is made from into long chains. The chains are then broken down into solid plastic pellets.

Finished product

The final product is a bright plastic toy duck that floats and will last for many years.

Melting down

The pellets are melted into liquid plastic. Other chemicals and colours are added to make different types of plastic.

Shaping objects

The plastic is poured into a hollow mould and air is blown in to make the plastic stick to the walls. It cools to become a solid plastic duck.

What makes fireworks explode?

When two substances meet they sometimes react – they might start to fizz or change to create something new. This is called a chemical reaction. Some chemical reactions produce explosions. The beautiful explosions of colour we see in fireworks are made by chemical reactions.

Colours

Fireworks have metal chemicals added to them so they glow different colours. Lithium produces red fireworks and sodium salts create yellow ones.

Where else do we see chemical reactions?

Apple turning brown
The insides of an apple start to turn brown in a chemical reaction with oxygen in the air.

Metal rusting
Iron reacts with water and oxygen in the air to make a reddish-brown substance called rust.

Making a bang
Fire travelling through a firework causes chemical reactions inside it. These reactions create the explosions people enjoy watching.

4. When the fire reaches the gunpowder, there is a huge explosion of heat, light, and colour.

3. The firework burns until the fire reaches the main chamber, which contains gunpowder mixed with metal chemicals.

Main chamber

2. The gunpowder explodes, releasing enough energy to launch the firework into the air.

1. The fuse is lit. It burns slowly until it reaches a first, small amount of gunpowder.

Fuse

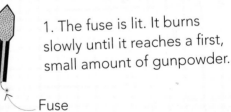

? True or false?

1. When you bake a cake, a chemical reaction takes place.

2. Burning fuel is a type of chemical reaction.

3. Not all fireworks use chemical reactions.

See pages 132–133 for the answers

Why is lemon juice sour?

Lemon juice tastes sour because it contains citric acid. Acids make things taste sharp or sour. Strong acids are dangerous and can burn through metal. Weak acids are safe to eat and drink.

The sourest thing in the natural world is the gooseberry.

What is a pH scale?

We measure acid on a scale called the pH scale. The lower the number, the more strongly acidic it is. At the other end of the scale are alkalis. If the number is higher than seven, the liquid is an alkali.

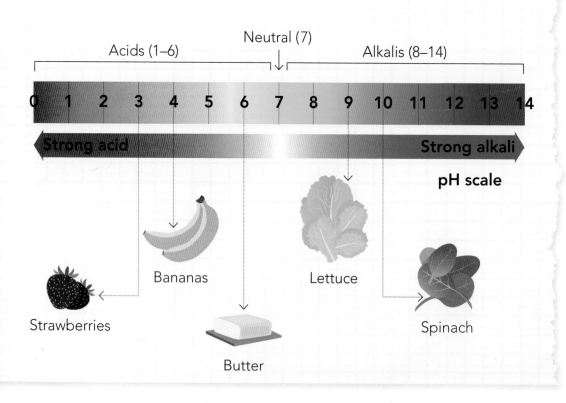

Neutral (7)

Acids (1–6)   Alkalis (8–14)

0 1 2 3 4 5 6 7 8 9 10 11 12 13 14

Strong acid   Strong alkali

pH scale

Strawberries

Bananas

Butter

Lettuce

Spinach

Sharp taste

Lemon juice contains high levels of citric acid, which has a pH value of 2. This gives lemons their strong, sharp taste.

What other foods are acidic?

Tinned tomatoes

Tinned tomatoes have a pH level of 3.5. Tomatoes contain a mixture of weak acids, which are safe to eat.

Vinegar

Vinegar contains acetic acid, which gives it a pH level of 3. It is used to add a sour flavour to food.

? True or false?

1. Lemons are more acidic than vinegar.

2. If we add an alkali to an acid we can make salt.

3. We can check if something is acid or alkali using litmus paper.

See pages 132–133 for the answers

Energy

Anything that moves has energy. It is power to make work happen. Energy can change from movement to electricity and then to heat and light.

Potential energy

When water is kept behind the wall of a dam, it has potential energy. Gravity is pulling the water down so it is ready to move when it is released.

Movement energy

When water is released from behind the wall of the dam, its potential energy changes into movement energy.

The Sun creates as much energy as 100 million billion coal-burning power stations.

Where does energy go?

Energy cannot be created or destroyed – it just changes from one type of energy to another. Stored energy in the food we eat changes into movement energy in our bodies. Movement energy in water can change into electrical energy in a light bulb.

What other forms of energy exist?

Chemical energy
Energy can be released during a chemical reaction. The energy stored in wood is released by burning it.

Nuclear energy
Nuclear energy is made when tiny particles called atoms are split apart in machines called nuclear reactors.

Changing energy

Movement energy can be converted into electricity using a generator. Electrical energy then changes into heat and light energy in a light bulb.

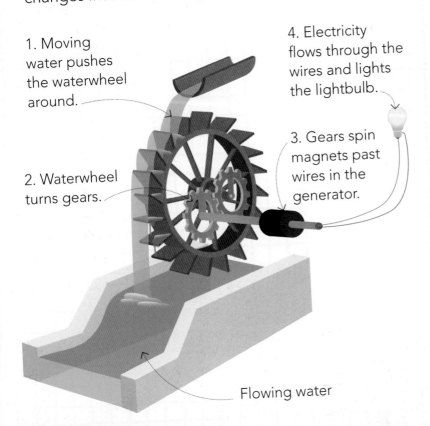

1. Moving water pushes the waterwheel around.

4. Electricity flows through the wires and lights the lightbulb.

3. Gears spin magnets past wires in the generator.

2. Waterwheel turns gears.

Flowing water

? Quick quiz

1. Where does most of the energy on planet Earth come from?

2. What do we call energy made from fuel that won't run out?

3. What type of energy is created when atoms are split apart?

See pages 132–133 for the answers

How do we see colours?

When we see colours, it is because light is bouncing off things and into our eyes. Some colours of light are absorbed by objects and some are reflected back. So, if something looks yellow, it's because yellow light is reflecting into our eyes.

Visible spectrum

The different colours we can see are called the visible spectrum. White light from the Sun is all the colours of light mixed together.

What is colour blindness?

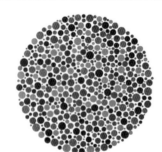

Red-green colour blindness

The most common type of colour blindness is red-green. If you have this you can't tell the difference between red and green.

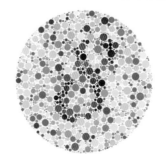

Blue-yellow colour blindness

Another type of colour blindness is blue-yellow. If you have this you can't see the difference between purple and yellow.

Sunlight

Our main source of light is the Sun. It takes eight minutes for light from the Sun to reach Earth.

Splitting light

If we pass white light through a prism it splits into all the colours of the rainbow. Colours come from light – all the colours are already inside the "white" light.

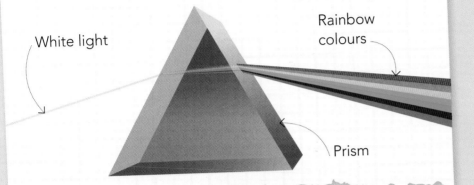

White light

Rainbow colours

Prism

Reflection

Yellow light is reflected into the eye by the flower petals. Sensors in the eye tell the brain that the object is yellow.

Absorption

All the colours from the Sun except yellow have been absorbed by the petals. Only the yellow reflects back towards the eye.

? Picture quiz

What is a shadow?

See pages 132–133 for the answer

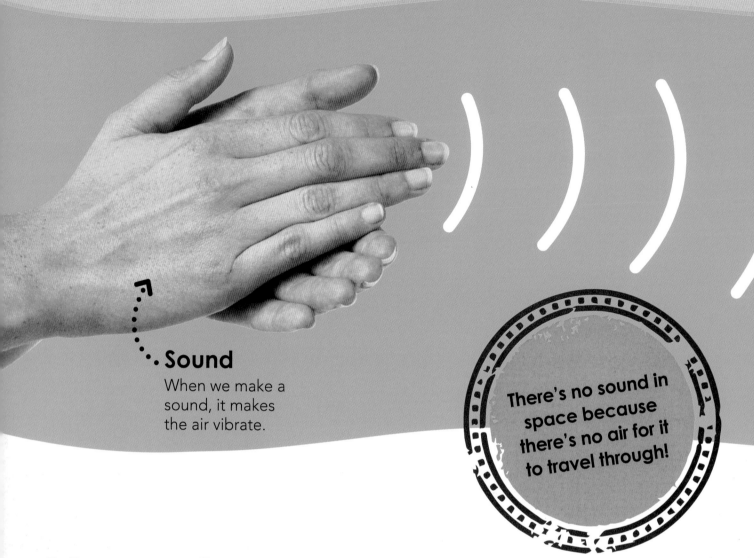

Sound

When we make a
sound, it makes
the air vibrate.

There's no sound in
space because
there's no air for it
to travel through!

How does sound move?

Sound is a vibration. It can travel through a solid, liquid, or gas. When we hear a sound, it's because vibrations have travelled through the air in waves called sound waves. These vibrations are picked up by our ears.

How humans hear

Sound waves travel into your ear. They vibrate a part of the ear called the ear drum. It passes vibrations through tiny bones, and then through a liquid. Sensors send the sound to the brain.

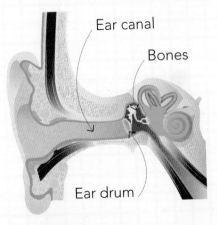

Ear canal

Bones

Ear drum

Inside of the ear

Sound waves

As sound travels, it vibrates the air by squashing and unsquashing it. This moving air is called a sound wave.

Sensing sounds

Our ears collect sound waves. They change sound vibrations into electrical signals that travel to the brain. Then the brain tells us what the sound is.

? Quick quiz

1. Can sound travel through solid materials?

2. Why does a bee buzz when it flies?

3. When we speak, what part of the body vibrates to make the sound?

See pages 132–133 for the answers

How do animals use echoes?

Underwater

Dolphins send clicking sounds through the water. The sounds bounce off things and help the dolphins find potential food.

In the dark

Bats send out pulses of sound, which bounce off objects. This stops bats from flying into walls, and helps them catch insects in the dark.

How does heat move?

Heat is always moving in one direction, from warm to cold. When we touch a warm object, heat moves into our skin. When we touch a cold object, heat moves out of our skin and into the object.

Hot water rises

Conduction

When we heat a pan of water, heat moves from the lower part of the pan to the upper part, heating the water in the process. When heat moves through solid objects we call it conduction.

What happens when lava (liquid rock) cools?

Lava bombs
Volcanoes throw out blobs of lava that cool as they move through the air. They become solid, making rocks.

Pillow lava
When lava enters the cold ocean it sometimes cools to make pillow-like shapes.

Convection

The water at the bottom of the pan heats up and rises and the colder water sinks. This heat movement in liquid or air is called convection.

The Sun

The Sun is our main source of heat. It warms the planet with invisible rays called radiation. When these rays shine on an object, they warm it up.

Cool water sinks

Sun

The Sun's rays

Earth

Radiation

Heat waves come from burning objects, heating the things they reach. This is called radiation.

? Quick quiz

1. What type of heat travels through the air from a fire?

2. What is the name for the way that heat travels through solid objects?

3. What happens when a solid is heated and becomes a liquid?

See pages 132–133 for the answers

What is electricity?

Electricity is a movement of energy – a flow of tiny, charged particles called electrons. Electrons can be charged up naturally in something called static electricity. Or we can make electricity from heat, light, wind, and other forms of energy.

Lightning

Lightning is a giant spark of electric charge that moves between the clouds and the ground, or between the clouds in the sky.

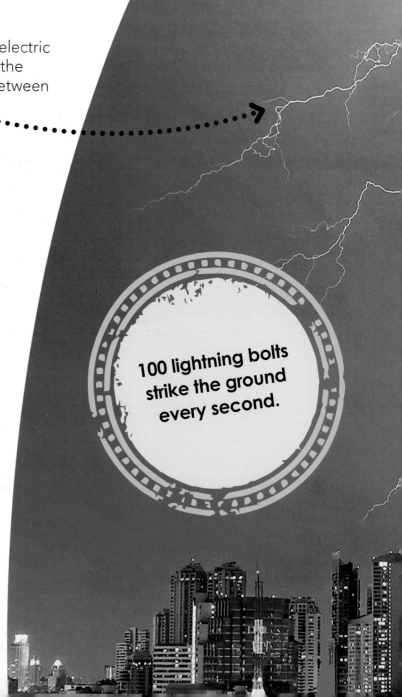

100 lightning bolts strike the ground every second.

How can we make electricity?

Solar energy
Solar panels use energy from the Sun to make electricity. They are often placed on house roofs.

Wind energy
Wind turbines use the movement of the wind to make electricity. A group of wind turbines is called a wind farm.

Water energy
Dams use the movement of water to turn turbines that make electricity.

Charged particles

All electricity is made from moving charged particles called electrons. These electrons flow as an electric current.

Clouds

Tiny bits of ice, rain, or snow in the clouds rub against each other, charging up static electricity. Eventually the charge leaps as lightning.

? Quick quiz

1. What are materials called that let electricity flow through them?

2. What is a lightning strike made from?

3. What type of electricity do you make by rubbing a balloon on your head?

See pages 132–133 for the answers

Battery

Batteries are a type of power source that store electricity. They have positive and negative ends. Both ends need to be connected to let electric current flow.

How do lights turn on?

When we use a light switch, electricity flows from a power source, through wires, and into a bulb that gives out light. The switch completes a loop of wires called a circuit. A circuit allows electric current to flow to the light, turning it on.

Wires

Electric current can only flow if the circuit makes a complete loop. Wires connect the circuit. They are usually made from copper.

Switch

The switch controls when electricity flows through the circuit. When the switch is open, it breaks the circuit and electric current can't flow.

Electricity moves at 200,000 km (125,000 miles) per second. That's two-thirds as fast as the fastest thing ever – light.

What are circuits used for?

Television sets
Tiny circuits inside television sets allow us to control things like brightness and volume.

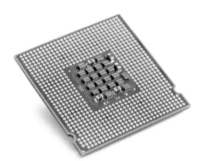

Mobile phones
Miniature circuits smaller than a fingernail are found in mobile phones and other electronic devices. These circuits are called microchips.

Light bulb
The light bulb glows when electric current passes through it. This is only a small light bulb, but all light bulbs everywhere are lit up in the same way.

Circuit diagram
Every component (object) in the circuit can be shown with a symbol. The wires are shown with straight lines.

Electricity flows around the circuit.

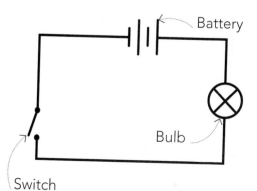

Battery

Bulb

Switch

Diagram of a simple circuit

? Picture quiz

This symbol shows a part of a circuit that breaks when too much electricity flows through the wires. What is it?

See pages 132–133 for the answer

How can I make my hair stand on end?

If you rub a balloon on your hair you can charge it with a safe amount of a type of electricity called static electricity. Tiny particles called electrons move from your hair to the balloon, charging it up and attracting your hair towards the balloon.

Electrons

Electrons are tiny, negatively charged particles. They are part of the atoms that everything is made of. When electrons flow they make electricity.

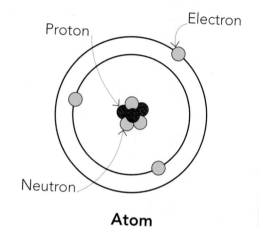

Proton

Electron

Neutron

Atom

How is static electricity useful?

Photocopier
Photocopiers use static electricity to stick negatively charged black ink onto positively charged areas of the page.

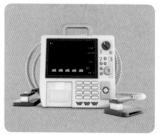

Defibrillator
Machines called defibrillators use static electricity to restart hearts that have stopped beating.

Giant sparks of static electricity that leap from the clouds are called lightning.

Negatively charged

The balloon becomes negatively charged when it is rubbed on the hair. This is because electrons are rubbed off the hair and onto the balloon.

See pages 132–133 for the answers

Positively charged

If something loses electrons it becomes positively charged. As electrons leave the hair and move onto the balloon the hair becomes positively charged.

Opposites attract

Opposite charges attract. The negatively charged balloon is attracted to the positively charged hair and they stick to each other.

Can you make electricity from a magnet?

If you move a magnet past a coil of wire, it makes electricity flow in the wire. Generators are machines that spin coils of wires past magnets or magnets past coils of wire to create electricity.

Powering up

As the rider pushes the pedals, the bike wheels turn. The front wheel turns the cog on the dynamo generator.

What else are magnets used for?

Scrap metal

Cranes with magnets on them can pick up magnetic metals such as iron from piles of rubbish.

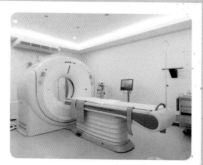

MRI

MRI stands for magnetic resonance imaging. MRI scanners can take pictures of the human brain.

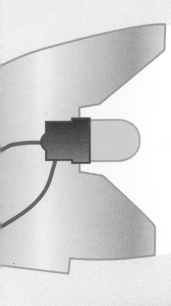

Lighting up

The dynamo generator makes enough electricity to power the light.

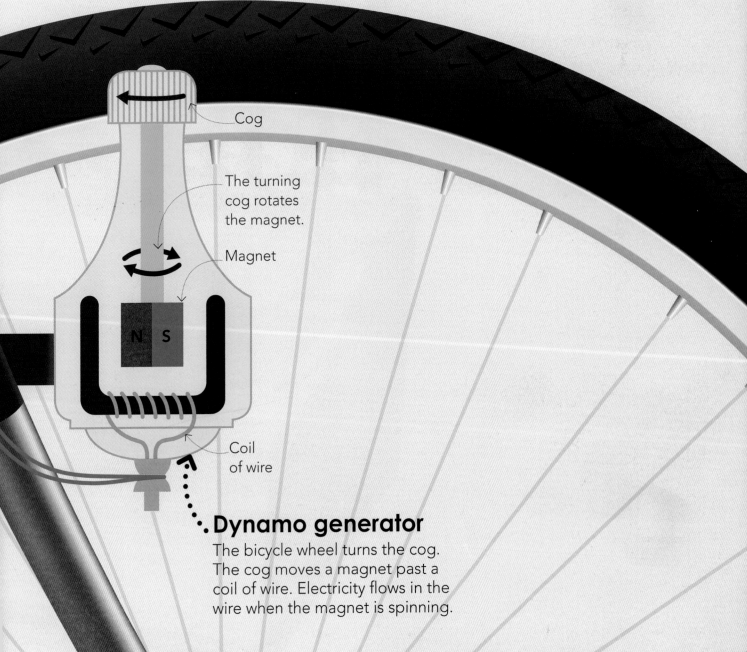

Cog

The turning cog rotates the magnet.

Magnet

N S

Coil of wire

Dynamo generator

The bicycle wheel turns the cog. The cog moves a magnet past a coil of wire. Electricity flows in the wire when the magnet is spinning.

Where does coal come from?

Coal is a fuel made from the remains of ancient plants that have been squashed underground. Coal burns easily and releases energy as heat and light. It can be burned in a power station to make electricity.

Coal and diamonds are made from the same thing – carbon.

1. Swamp

Trees, ferns, and moss die and sink into the swamp. New plants grow and die, and the layers pile into the swamp.

? Quick quiz

1. What is the group name for coal, oil, and gas?

2. Where is coal formed?

3. What is the name of a place where we dig out coal?

See pages 132–133 for the answers

What other fuels form underground?

Crude oil

Oil is made from tiny plants and animals called plankton that lived in the oceans millions of years ago. They died and got buried under mud and squashed into oil.

Natural gas

Natural gas was formed in the same way and at the same time in the past as oil. It also comes from plankton. Natural gas and crude oil are often found together underground.

2. Burial

Earth builds up over the swamp, pushing down and squeezing the plant layer. As it gets squashed it heats up.

3. Coal

Over time, the layers get squashed and heat up further. Gases are forced out and the plants become layers of coal.

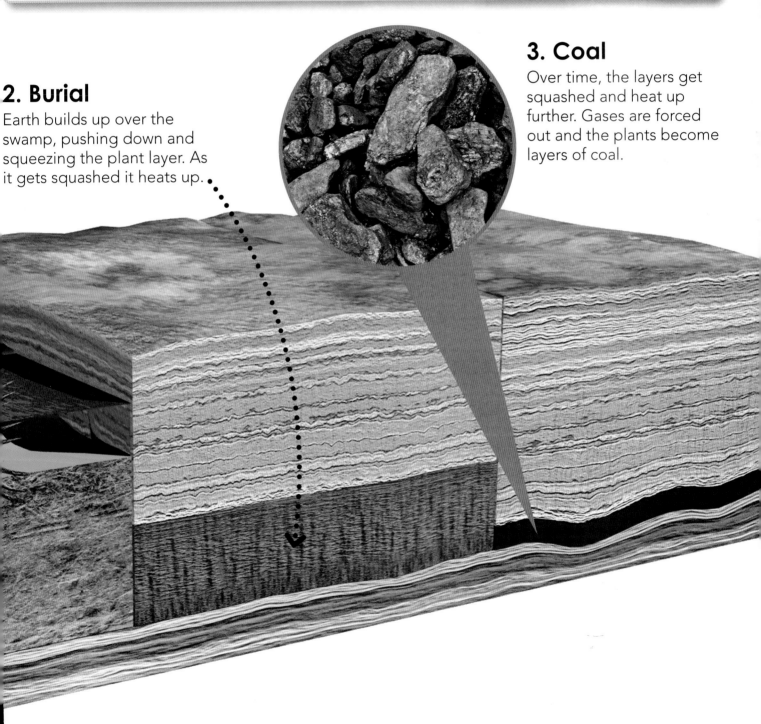

Forces and movement

Forces are pushes and pulls that act on objects.
They make things speed up or slow down. They
can lift things into the air or move them around.

What makes things speed up or slow down?

A British scientist called Isaac Newton discovered three laws of motion that help us to understand how objects behave when forces push or pull on them. Forces make things speed up or slow down.

FIRST LAW

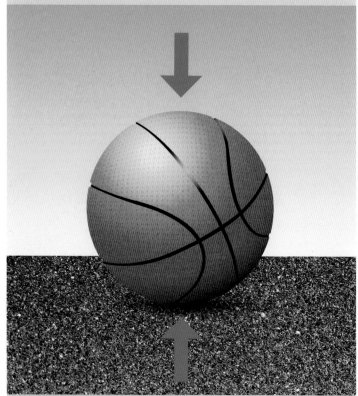

Stationary ball

When forces are balanced, an object stays at rest or, if it is moving, it keeps moving at a constant speed. Objects only change speed when extra force is added.

SECOND LAW

Getting faster

If we push the basketball forward with our hands, the extra force we give it makes it speed up and move in the direction we pushed it in.

What helps animals move fast?

Strength
A cheetah is fast because it is light with strong, powerful legs. Its feet have good grips, which let it push off from the ground as it runs.

Smooth shape
A penguin moves quickly through the water because its body is shaped a bit like a lemon, allowing it to move through water easily. This is called streamlining.

THIRD LAW

Bouncing back
For every action there is an equal and opposite reaction. If the ball pushes into a wall at speed, the wall will push the ball back the opposite way.

Acceleration means to speed up.

? True or false?

1. In space, moving objects can keep moving forever as there is no air to slow them down.

2. An object moving through air is slowed down by air pushing it back.

3. When forces are balanced an object moves slowly.

See pages 132–133 for the answers

What stops things slipping?

Friction is a force that acts between two surfaces that are moving or trying to move. It slows things down. For example, there is friction between the soles of our shoes and the ground when we walk.

If you rub your hands together, the friction between them will start to produce heat.

How friction works

As two surfaces move past each other they rub, slowing each other down. Friction always acts in the opposite direction to movement.

Friction produced between the surfaces

Two surfaces moving past each other

Which shoes are supposed to slip?

Skis
The bottom surfaces of skis are smooth, reducing friction, so they glide easily over the snow. The snow and ice below each ski melt to reduce friction even more, making travelling faster.

Tap shoes
The soles of tap-dancing shoes are made of polished metal. This means that there is much less friction between the shoe and the ground, so tap dancers can glide around when dancing.

Rough surface
Rough surfaces increase friction. Wet, icy, or muddy surfaces reduce it, so cars are more likely to skid in these conditions.

? True or false?

1. Friction helps a footballer kick a football in the right direction.

2. Friction between the air and an aeroplane is called air resistance.

3. Rough surfaces produce more friction than smooth surfaces.

See pages 132–133 for the answers

Great grip
Tyres have treads on the bottom of them to increase friction, so they can grip the road or track.

How do magnets pull?

Magnets have two poles, a north and south pole. There is an invisible force field between the poles called the magnetic field. Magnetic metals and other magnets are attracted towards a magnet when they enter its magnetic field.

South pole
South poles pull north poles towards them and push other south poles away.

North pole
North poles pull south poles towards them and push other north poles away.

What are magnets used for?

Transport
Maglev, short for magnetic levitation, trains are one of the fastest train services on Earth. Powerful magnets on the tracks let the trains hover a few millimetres above the rails.

Navigation
A compass is used to find the way using the Earth's magnetic field. The magnetic needle in the compass always points in the direction of north.

Earth's magnetic field

The Earth has a magnetic field that protects us from harmful rays from outer space. The Earth's North and South poles are where the Earth's magnetic field is strongest.

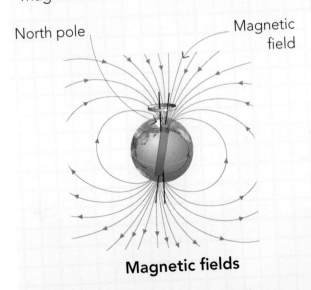

North pole

Magnetic field

Magnetic fields

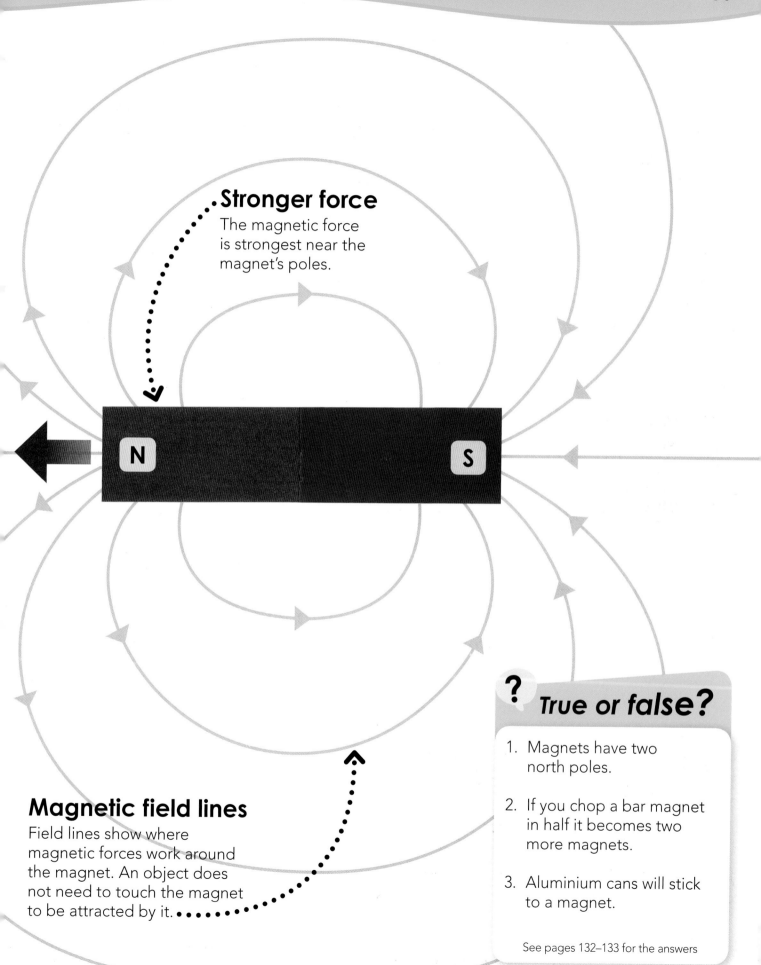

Stronger force
The magnetic force is strongest near the magnet's poles.

N   S

Magnetic field lines
Field lines show where magnetic forces work around the magnet. An object does not need to touch the magnet to be attracted by it.

? True or false?

1. Magnets have two north poles.

2. If you chop a bar magnet in half it becomes two more magnets.

3. Aluminium cans will stick to a magnet.

See pages 132–133 for the answers

How can I move something more easily?

Machines help us to move things more easily. A machine is something that makes a push or pull bigger, or helps to change the direction that it acts in. Levers, pulleys, and gears are simple machines.

The first ever machine was a wedge-shaped axe from the Stone Age.

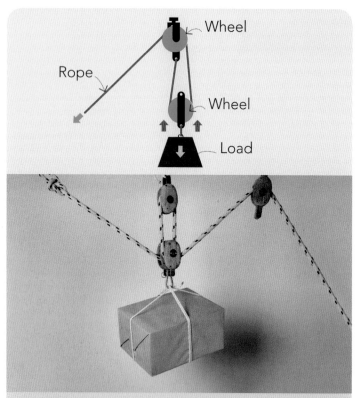

Pulley

A pulley cuts down the effort it takes to lift a heavy weight. The more pulleys you add, the easier it gets to lift.

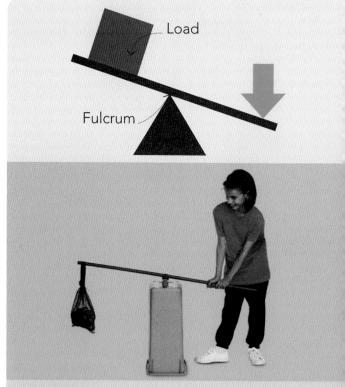

Lever

Levers make it easier to move things. A small push force has a bigger impact at the other end of the lever than just lifting would.

? True or false?

1. A door handle is an example of a lever.

2. Crows can use levers.

3. A screw is a simple machine.

See pages 132–133 for the answers

What are some other types of simple machines?

Screw

A screw changes the direction of a force. It changes a turning movement into a forward push. As you turn the screw, it pushes down.

Wheelbarrow

Most of a wheelbarrow's load is carried by the wheel and axle. This makes carrying heavy loads easier.

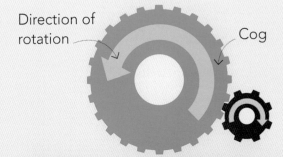

Direction of rotation   Cog

Gears

Gears can change the direction and speed of a rotation. Turning pedals on a bicycle moves the wheels around using gears.

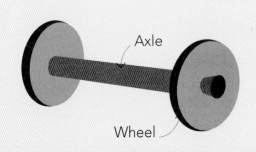

Axle

Wheel

Wheel and axle

A wheel is a turning machine that makes moving objects along the ground easier. Axles join pairs of wheels together.

What makes cars go?

Most cars use petrol for fuel. This is squashed inside a chamber in the engine. The fuel is lit and then explodes, pushing a piston that rotates a long pole called a crankshaft. As the crankshaft turns, it makes the wheels drive the car forwards.

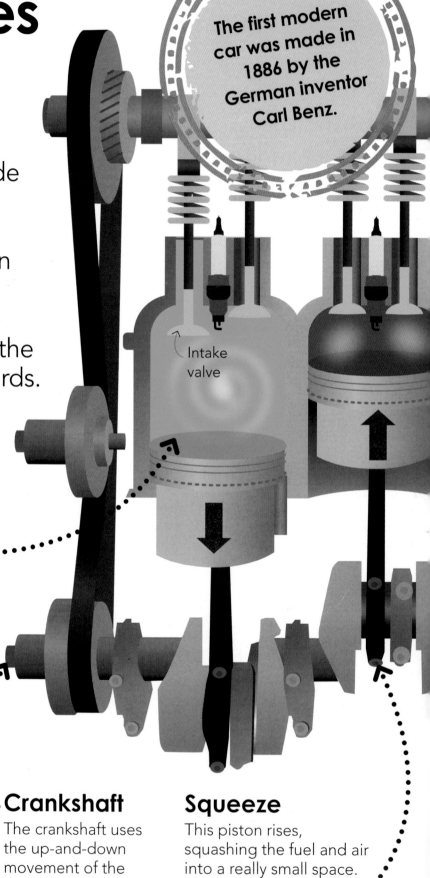

The first modern car was made in 1886 by the German inventor Carl Benz.

Intake valve

Fuel in
This piston moves down and fuel and air are sucked in. This happens once every time the crankshaft turns.

See pages 132–133 for the answers

? Quick quiz

1. How many cars currently exist in the world?

2. What happens to air and fuel when it gets squashed into a small space?

3. What are petrol and diesel made from?

Crankshaft
The crankshaft uses the up-and-down movement of the pistons to turn the wheels round.

Squeeze
This piston rises, squashing the fuel and air into a really small space. The air and fuel heat up as they get squashed.

Inside a car

Engines are usually at the front of a car. They move the front wheels to propel the car forwards and backwards. Four-wheel drive cars turn both sets of wheels.

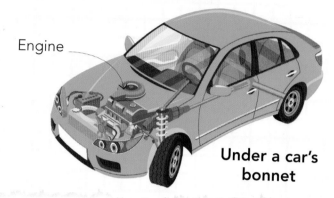

Engine

Under a car's bonnet

Spark plug

Exhaust valve

Waste out

When fuel burns it releases waste products. They are carbon dioxide gas, steam, and pollution. This piston pushes the waste out into the exhaust pipe.

Crankshaft rotation

Spark

A tiny electrical signal makes a spark light the squashed fuel and air. It explodes, pushing this piston down and turning the crankshaft.

How else can we power cars?

Diesel
Many older cars and some modern cars use a fuel called diesel to power the engine.

Electric car
Some modern cars use a combination of fuel and electricity, while others run completely on electricity.

What stops us floating away?

There is an invisible force constantly pulling us down towards the Earth. This force is called gravity. When we throw a ball up it comes down because of gravity. Gravity stops us floating off into space.

We move at a constant speed or stay still until a force slows us down or speeds us up.

Lift-off

The skateboarder pushes away from the ground, pushing against the force of gravity to lift off.

Upward force

Going up

As the skateboarder moves into the air, the force of gravity slows him down until he stops moving upwards.

Where else do we see gravity at work?

Solar system

The planets move in circles around our star, the Sun. They are kept in place by the force of gravity. Large objects, such as stars, pull smaller objects, such as planets, towards them.

Landslides

Landslides happen on slopes. When earth or rocks become unstable, they start to slip and move down the slope. This happens because of the pulling force of gravity.

Falling down

The skateboarder begins to move downwards, speeding up as gravity pulls him down. This is called acceleration.

Gravity

Safe landing

The ground stops the downward acceleration and the skateboarder lands. He bends his legs to cushion the upward force from the ground.

? Quick quiz

1. How does the force of gravity change between take-off and landing?

2. What is it called when something speeds up?

3. If forces are balanced on an object, what will it do?

See pages 132–133 for the answers

Propeller engine

As the propeller spins, it pushes air out backwards, faster than when it comes in. This creates a force called thrust that pushes the aeroplane forwards.

How do planes stay in the air?

As a plane moves forwards, air rushes over its wings and down towards the ground. As the plane gets faster, the downward push of the air is strong enough to lift the whole aeroplane up into the air.

? Quick quiz

1. How does wing shape make aeroplanes lift up?

2. What force acts the opposite way to lift?

3. What is the job of the tailplane?

See pages 132–133 for the answers

Tail

The tailplane works like a mini wing. It stops the aeroplane rotating, keeping it stable in the air.

How do rockets fly through the air?

Jet propulsion

When a rocket takes off, air rushes out of the bottom of the rocket. This pushes it upwards, in the opposite direction to the air's movement.

Lift

Direction of wind

Pressure exerted by slow-moving air

A plane's wings are shaped to push air down. This shape is called an aerofoil.

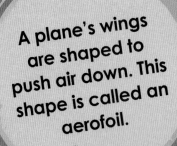

Wings

The wing shape pushes the air rushing past downwards. The force of air going down pushes the plane up in the opposite direction. This is called lift.

Flying forces

There are four main forces acting on a flying plane: drag, lift, thrust, and weight.

Thrust is the forward push of the aeroplane. It is created by air rushing away in the opposite direction.

Lift is the force that lifts the aeroplane up and off the ground. It is made by the wings forcing air downwards.

Thrust

Lift

Drag

Weight

Weight is the constant downward force of gravity acting on the plane.

Drag is the force of the air slowing down the aeroplane. It is the opposite of thrust.

Our planet

We live on a rocky planet, orbiting a star, in a Universe mostly made of empty space. Earth is the only planet known to have the perfect conditions for life.

True or false?

1. The Earth's crust is split into giant jigsaw pieces that move around.

2. You could dig a hole into the Earth's core.

3. The Earth's core is hotter than the Sun.

See pages 132–133 for the answers

Crust

The crust is the solid rock layer that makes up the surface of the Earth on land and at the bottom of the oceans.

If the Earth were the size of an apple, the crust would be as thick as an apple's skin.

Life below ground

Animals such as centipedes live in soil in the crust. They burrow in the soil, mixing it around.

Mantle

The thickest layer is the mantle. It is made from hot rock. The upper part is liquid called magma. The lower part is solid rock.

What rock is the crust made from?

Granite

The crust under land is mostly made from granite. It has mountains, soil, and buildings on top of it.

Basalt

The thinner crust of the ocean floor is mostly made from basalt. It has sand and sea water on top of it.

Inner core

The inner core is made from hot, solid iron and nickel. It is squashed into a solid by all the layers above it.

Outer core

The outer core is made from liquid nickel and iron metal.

How deep can a hole get?

We can only dig into the top layer of the Earth – the crust. If we could dig through the planet's layers, we'd travel through soil, solid rock, hot rock, liquid metal, then finally arrive at the solid metal core at the centre of the Earth.

Why does the ground shake?

Huge pieces of rock called plates make up the surface of the Earth. These plates move around, and sometimes get stuck as they try to move past each other. When rock moves suddenly, the ground shakes, creating an earthquake.

Earth's plates move a few centimetres every year. This is the same speed fingernails grow.

? Quick quiz

1. Which machines are used to measure earthquakes?

2. What is the name of the scale used to measure earthquakes?

3. What are the three main ways tectonic plates move?

See pages 132–133 for the answers

Fault lines

Cracks along large areas of rock are called faults. They can be massive plate boundaries or smaller cracks in other places.

Types of plate boundaries

Boundaries are areas where huge slabs of rock meet and move.
Plates move in three different ways at these boundaries.

Plates pulling away from each other.

Plates push towards each other.

Liquid rock flows out between the plates.

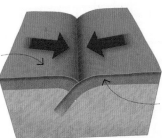

Plates slide past each other.

Tremors occur where plates rub against each other.

One plate is forced below the other.

Apart

Together

Along

Bendy rock

Rock can stretch and bend as it moves. Sometimes it springs back into place, making the Earth shake.

Where do earthquakes happen?

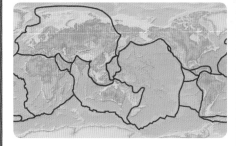

Plate boundaries

Earth's surface is broken into huge chunks of rock called tectonic plates. Most earthquakes happen in places where the tectonic plates rub together.

Where does rain come from?

Water is constantly moving between the land, rivers, air, and the ocean in something called the water cycle. The Sun's heat drives the water cycle. It makes water from the oceans rise into the air and eventually fall as rain.

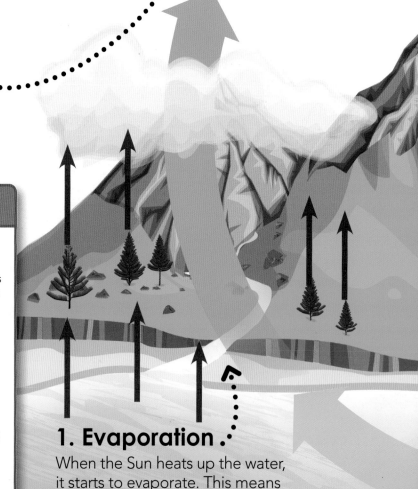

2. Condensation

As it rises, water vapour starts to cool and begins to turn back to tiny water droplets and make clouds. This is called condensation.

Is all water the same?

Fresh water

Fresh water is the water we drink. Rain is fresh water. We find it in lakes, streams, and rivers, underground, and in ice.

Salt water

Salt water is found in oceans and seas. It tastes salty compared to fresh water. Salt water makes up 97.5 per cent of the water on planet Earth.

1. Evaporation

When the Sun heats up the water, it starts to evaporate. This means it changes from a liquid to a gas. The gas is called water vapour.

3. Precipitation

Rain, snow, or hail fall from the clouds when the tiny droplets get heavier than the air around them. This is called precipitation.

? Picture quiz

What happens when there is a shortage of water?

See pages 132–133 for the answer

4. Run-off

Rain water trickles into streams that flow into rivers, which then carry the rain towards the sea.

5. Back to the sea

The water returns to the sea, or is collected in lakes, where the sun heats it and the whole cycle begins again.

Why is planet Earth blue?

More than two-thirds of the Earth's surface is covered in water, making our planet look blue from space. The huge oceans hide deep trenches, volcanoes, and mountain ranges. They are home to a great variety of living things.

Oceans of the world

There are five oceans on Earth. Smaller seas, gulfs, and bays are parts of the oceans, usually near the land. The Earth's oceans produce more than two-thirds of the oxygen we breathe, through tiny plants called phytoplankton.

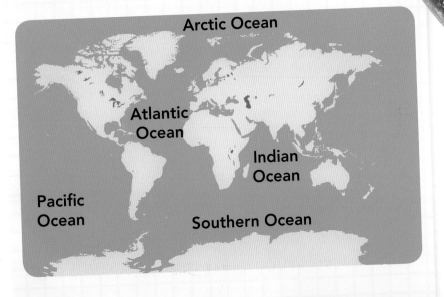

Arctic Ocean

Atlantic Ocean

Indian Ocean

Pacific Ocean

Southern Ocean

Clouds

Images of Earth taken from space show swirling white clouds in the atmosphere.

We have mapped more of the surface of Venus than we have the oceans of Earth.

? True or false?

1. The largest ocean is the Atlantic.

2. The deepest part of the ocean is 11 km (7 miles) below the surface.

3. During the winter, the Arctic Ocean is almost completely covered in ice.

See pages 132–133 for the answers

Pacific Ocean

The Pacific is the largest ocean on Earth, coving one-third of the planet's surface.

How deep is the ocean?

Sunlight zone
The sunlight zone goes from the surface to around 200 m (650 ft)deep. It's a bright area where we find coral reefs and colourful fish.

Twilight zone
The twilight zone goes from around 200 m (650 ft) to 1,000 m (3,300 ft) deep. It's darker than the sunlight zone.

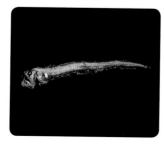

Midnight zone
The midnight zone goes from 1,000 m (3,300 ft) to 4,000 m (13,000 ft) deep. It is completely dark apart from tiny lights made by sea creatures.

Where does wind come from?

The Sun heats up the surface of planet Earth. The land heats up faster than water so the air above land is warmer than the air above the sea. Warm air rises and cooler air sinks. This movement of air is called wind.

Weather patterns

Cold air from the North and South Poles sinks towards the warm equator, the imaginary line around the centre of the Earth. The Earth's surface near the equator is spun faster than the poles so the wind ends up moving towards the west.

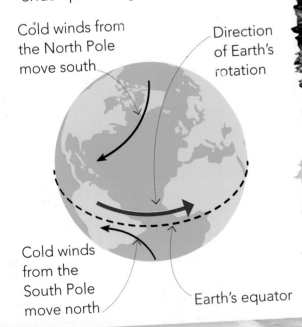

Cold winds from the North Pole move south

Direction of Earth's rotation

Cold winds from the South Pole move north

Earth's equator

Land air

The warm air above the land rises because it is less squashed together than colder air. Warm air floats above colder air.

Quick quiz

1. Why is the air above land warmer than the air above the sea?

2. What is the name we give to the fastest type of wind?

3. What is the scale we measure wind on?

See pages 132–133 for the answers

How can we keep track of the wind?

Wind sock

A wind sock is an instrument that shows the direction the wind is blowing towards. The hollow tube is lifted as the wind blows through it. Wind socks are used at airports.

Anemometer

An anemometer is a machine that measures wind speed. Little cups catch the wind and spin around. The faster the wind moves, the faster they turn.

Flow of air

As the warm air rises it starts to cool and form clouds, which move out to sea.

Sinking air

Cold, wet air sinks because it is heavier and closer together than warmer air. When it meets the sea it stops sinking.

Sea breeze

Cool air is sucked towards the land where the warm air has risen up. This movement is called the onshore breeze.

What's inside a hurricane?

Hurricanes are massive, swirling storms full of clouds, wind, and rain. Hurricanes form when thunderstorms meet over warm ocean waters. At the centre of a hurricane is a calm area called the eye of the storm.

Icy clouds

Clouds overflow from the centre to make a layer of thin, icy clouds on top. It moves in the opposite direction to the clouds underneath.

Ocean waters

Hurricanes occur where seas are at least 200 ft (60 m) deep and at least 27°C (80°F) warm.

How do hurricanes affect us?

Damage
Hurricane winds are so strong they can blow down buildings and destroy electricity and water supplies. This can leave people without homes, schools, and places to go to work.

Flooding
Hurricane winds can create massive waves that flood towns on the coast. During a hurricane, a month's worth of rain can fall in a few hours.

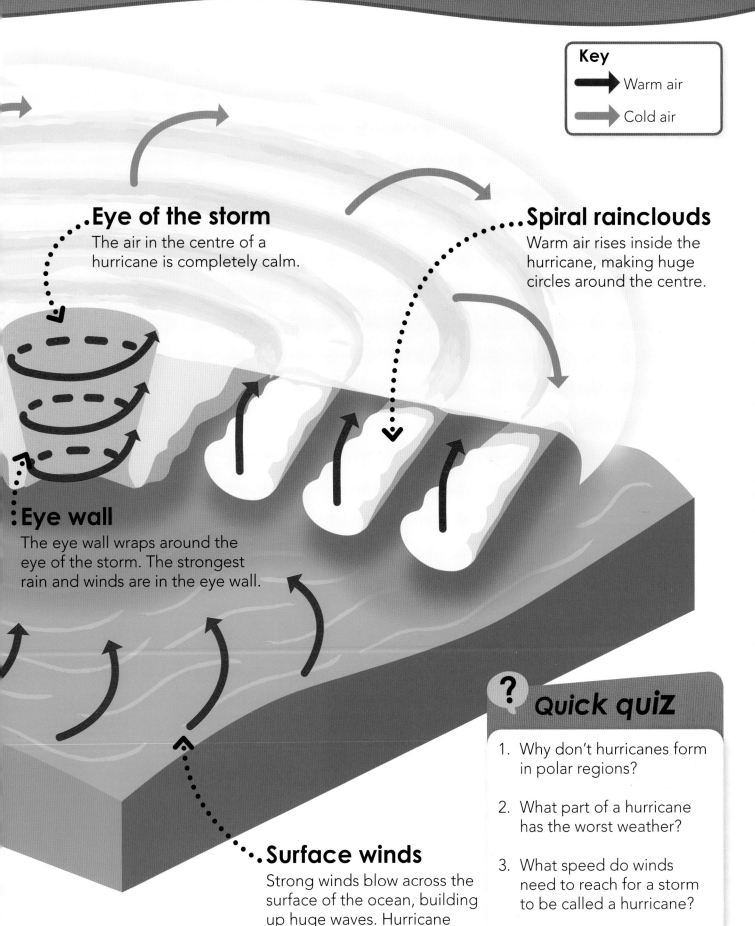

Key
→ Warm air
→ Cold air

Eye of the storm
The air in the centre of a hurricane is completely calm.

Spiral rainclouds
Warm air rises inside the hurricane, making huge circles around the centre.

Eye wall
The eye wall wraps around the eye of the storm. The strongest rain and winds are in the eye wall.

Surface winds
Strong winds blow across the surface of the ocean, building up huge waves. Hurricane winds blow at over 120 km (73 miles) an hour.

? Quick quiz

1. Why don't hurricanes form in polar regions?

2. What part of a hurricane has the worst weather?

3. What speed do winds need to reach for a storm to be called a hurricane?

See pages 132–133 for the answers

Where does planet Earth end?

Planet Earth is protected by layers of gases called the atmosphere. At around 100 km (62 miles) above sea level, the Earth's atmosphere ends and space begins. This is called the Karman line.

Orbiting satellite

Do other planets have atmospheres?

Jupiter
Jupiter is a planet made from gas. It has a thick atmosphere made up of hydrogen, helium, methane, and ammonia gases.

Mercury
Mercury is a rocky planet with low gravity and almost no atmosphere. Gases around Mercury are blown away by the Sun's solar wind.

Exosphere
This is the final layer of the atmosphere, where air completely runs out to become airless outer space.

Thermosphere
This layer is the last one before the atmosphere fades into space. The Karman line is in this layer. Temperatures can reach 2,000°C (3,600°F).

? True or false?

1. The atmosphere is held in place by gravity.

2. Earth is the only planet with an atmosphere.

3. The stratosphere has warmer layers higher up and cooler layers lower down.

See pages 132–133 for the answers

Exosphere
690–10,000 km
(430–6,200 miles)

Thermosphere
85–695 km
(53–430 miles)

Mesosphere

This is the coldest part of the Earth's atmosphere. It is where meteors break up before they can hit the Earth.

Stratosphere

The stratosphere includes the ozone layer. The Sun's rays bounce off the ozone layer, protecting the Earth.

Karman line
100 km (62 miles)

Meteors

Mesosphere
50–85 km
(30–53 miles)

Rockets

Aircraft

Stratosphere
20–50 km
(12–30 miles)

Ozone layer
20–30 km
(12–18 miles)

Troposphere
0–20 km
(0–12 miles)

Troposphere

This layer is where weather happens. It's the only layer where we can naturally breathe.

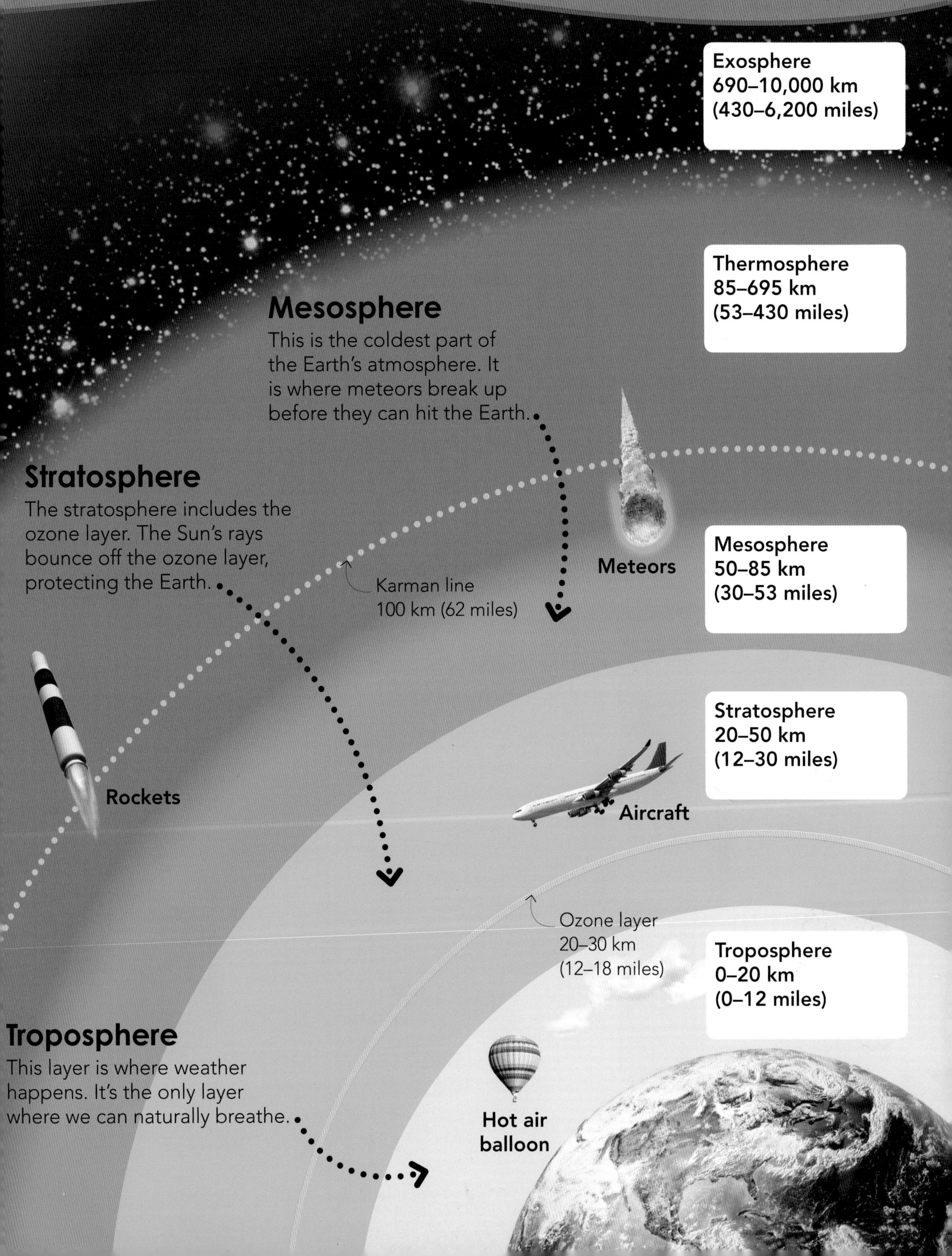

Hot air balloon

Where does the Moon go?

The Moon takes a month to travel around the Earth. Depending on where it is on that journey, different amounts of sunlight are reflected off the Moon's surface. Sometimes it seems to disappear altogether. In reality, though, the Moon is always there – we just can't always see sunlight reflecting off it.

Which other planets have moons?

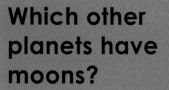

Jupiter
Jupiter has 53 moons. One moon, Io, has many active volcanoes on it. Another, called Europa, is covered in ice!

Saturn
Saturn has at least 53 moons. One of its moons, called Titan, is made from ice and rock and has a layer of gases around it.

Light and dark
The side of the Moon facing the Sun is lit up, while the other side facing away from the Sun is in shadow.

Lunar phases
The Moon appears to change shape during its monthly journey when seen from Earth.

From Earth, we only ever see the same side of the Moon.

Waning crescent

Last quarter

Waning gibbous

Sunlight

Reflected light

The Moon doesn't make light of its own. It only reflects the Sun's light.

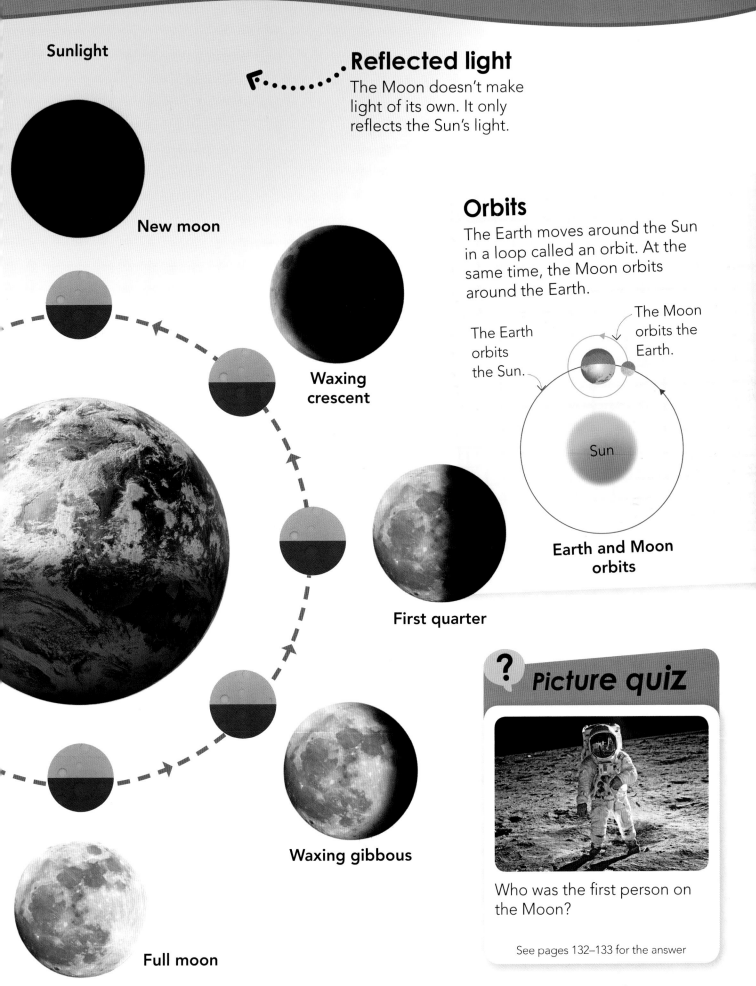

New moon

Orbits

The Earth moves around the Sun in a loop called an orbit. At the same time, the Moon orbits around the Earth.

The Earth orbits the Sun.

The Moon orbits the Earth.

Sun

Earth and Moon orbits

Waxing crescent

First quarter

Waxing gibbous

Full moon

?

Picture quiz

Who was the first person on the Moon?

See pages 132–133 for the answer

Can we live on other planets?

A planet needs the perfect ingredients and conditions for life to survive. Ingredients include liquid water, oxygen gas, and food. Conditions include the right temperature, protection from harmful rays, and the right amount of gravity.

Sun

Too hot

The thick, toxic atmosphere on Venus has trapped lots of heat, making this the hottest planet in the Solar System.

Venus

Hot and cold

Mercury is too hot for life on the side that faces the Sun and too cold the other side. It has no atmosphere.

Mercury

Earth

Mars

The red planet

Mars has very little atmosphere so the Sun's heat isn't trapped by gases. Instead, it just bounces back into space, making Mars too cold for life.

Perfect conditions

Earth has an atmosphere, liquid water, and the right level of gravity. It's in the "Goldilocks zone", which means it's not too hot and not too cold, but just right for life.

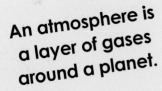

An atmosphere is a layer of gases around a planet.

Can distant planets support life?

Kepler 186f
This Earth-like planet has a rocky surface and may have water on it. But it would take 500 years to get to Kepler 186f, even if we could travel at the speed of light.

Kepler 452b
This planet is close in size to Earth and orbits a star similar to our Sun. It is in the "Goldilocks zone" of its solar system, but scientists do not yet know if it has water.

Gas giants
The four outer planets are made from gas so they don't have a solid surface. They are so massive that their gravity would squash us.

? Quick quiz

1. Which planet used to be similar to Earth?

2. Why don't we travel to planets outside of our solar system?

3. What are planets from outside our own solar system called?

See pages 132–133 for the answers

Jupiter

Saturn

Uranus

Neptune

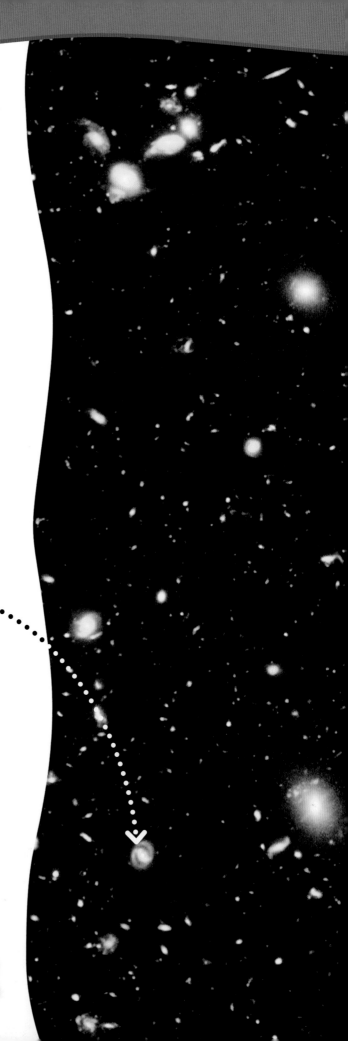

What is space made from?

Space is mostly a vast, silent, empty space. It looks dark because of huge gaps between objects that give out light, such as stars. Space is expanding all the time. We don't know where it ends or if it even has an end.

Galaxies

Groups of billions of stars are called galaxies. Galaxies have collapsed stars called black holes at their centre.

Dark matter

Scientists believe an invisible substance called dark matter and an invisible force called dark energy exist in space. Most of the Universe is made up of dark matter and energy.

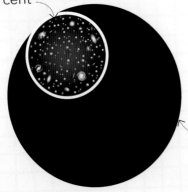

Visible matter
20 per cent

Dark matter and energy
80 per cent

If you could drive a car straight up in the air it would take about an hour to reach space.

? **True or false?**

1. There are more galaxies in the Universe then people on planet Earth.

2. Our star, the Sun, is about halfway through its life.

3. Space is mainly full of stars.

See pages 132–133 for the answers

How do we take photos of space?

Land-based telescopes

It is easier to build and fix telescopes on land than in space. Huge telescopes take detailed images of space.

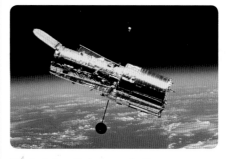

Hubble Space telescope

The Hubble telescope floats in space. It takes pictures of the Universe away from the light pollution found on Earth.

Stars

There are lots of different types of stars. Some are just being born and some are exploding at the end of their lives. They shine because they burn gases at hot temperatures.

How do people travel into space?

People first started travelling into space in the 1960s. They travelled in space rockets and later space shuttles. Earth's gravity pulls things down, so a space rocket needs to be powerful enough to escape gravity.

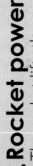
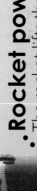

Capsule

The Soyuz capsule protects humans from the Sun's rays and from heat that is made when the rocket passes quickly through the Earth's atmosphere.

Rocket power

The rocket lifts the capsule into space and then separates from it and returns to Earth. Meanwhile, the capsule keeps travelling in space.

Inside the capsule

The rocket takes up to three astronauts and supplies to the International Space Station. Astronauts need to take food, water and air with them

What do people do in space?

Fix satellites

There are thousands of satellites travelling around the Earth. They help us to predict the weather and send phone, TV, and GPS signals.

Experiments

Astronauts visit the International Space Station, a huge space craft that was built in space. They live there for months and do science experiments.

Gantry arms

Gantry arms support the rocket and hold it upright before launch. They release the rocket during lift-off.

Boosters

Strap-on boosters power the rocket for lift-off. Gas shoots out of the bottom and the rocket is propelled upwards. The boosters fall away later.

The word astronaut means "star sailor".

Spacesuits

Space has no air in it, so people who travel outside a spacecraft need to take air with them. A space suit carries oxygen and protects the body from harmful space rays. It keeps the body at the right temperature in the extreme cold of space.

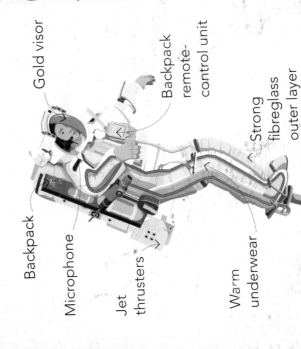

Gold visor

Backpack remote-control unit

Backpack

Microphone

Jet thrusters

Warm underwear

Strong fibreglass outer layer

? Quick quiz

1. Why is space food usually dry?

2. What was the first animal in space?

3. Why do rockets have to be so powerful?

See pages 132–133 for the answers

Answers

Page 7 1) False. Biology is the study of living things. 2) True.

Page 10 1) False. Giant tortoises can live for over 200 years, but ocean quahogs (a type of shellfish) can live for 500 years. 2) True. 3) True.

Page 13 Invertebrates.

Page 15 1) True. 2) False. Bacteria come in three shapes. 3) False. There are 100,000 bacteria on every sq cm (0.15 sq in) of your skin.

Page 17 1) True. 2) False. Plants need light to grow. 3) True.

Page 19 1) True. 2) True. 3) False. Spiders have tiny hair-like hooks on their feet.

Page 21 1) False. Most adult insects have wings, spiders don't. 2) True. 3) True.

Page 23 The ostrich.

Page 25 1) False. Some mammals live in the sea. 2) False. Mammals are the only animals that have fur on their bodies. 3) True.

Page 27 1) False. Female lions do most of the hunting. 2) True. 3) False. There are no wild lions in Australia – most live in Africa.

Page 29 1) True. 2) True. 3) True.

Page 31 1) False. Penguins live in the Antarctic, not the Arctic. 2) True. 3) False. Polar bears live in the Arctic.

Page 32 1) Fossils are very rare because most dead dinosaurs were eaten or rotted away. 2) Yes, they can be preserved inside amber, which comes from tree sap. 3) Coprolites.

Page 37 1) Red blood cells. 2) The digestive system. 3) The skin.

Page 39 1) True. 2) True. 3) True.

Page 41 1) 22 bones. 2) The hands. 3) Over 400 joints.

Page 43 1) True. 2) True. 3) False. Muscles only pull, they can't push.

Page 45 1) The oxygen we need comes from plants. 2) 23,000. 3) The trachea.

Page 47 1) True. 2) False. Blood cells are made inside bones. 3) True.

Page 48 1) Muscles in the intestines move the food along by squeezing it. 2) Sugar. 3) It takes one to three days for food to pass all the way through the body.

Page 51 1) Memories are stored and useless information is deleted. 2) Two hemispheres. 3) Ancient Egyptians removed the brain by pulling it out through the nose.

Page 53 1) False. The top layer of your skin is replaced every month. 2) True. 3) False. A group of tiny cuts is called a graze.

Page 55 1) White blood cells. 2) Tonsils catch and fight germs that enter the mouth. 3) Saliva kills germs.

Page 59 1) The neutron. 2) Nuclear energy. 3) Molecules.

Page 60 1) Solidifying. 2) A solid. 3) Mercury.

Page 63 1) No, saltwater can be deadly for humans to drink. 2) No, the water in rivers and lakes is fresh water. 3) Evaporation.

Page 65 Rust is formed.

Page 66 1) True. 2) False. Under 20 per cent of our plastic is recycled. 3) True.

Page 69 1) True. 2) True. 3) False. All fireworks use chemical reactions.

Page 71 1) True. 2) True. 3) True.

Page 75 1) The Sun.
2) Renewable energy.
3) Nuclear energy.

Page 77 A shadow is an area where light is blocked from reflecting off a surface by an object in the way of the light.

Page 79 1) Yes, sound can travel through solids, liquids, and gases. 2) The bee's wings are vibrating, making a buzzing sound. 3) The voice box.

Page 81 1) Radiation.
2) Conduction.
3) It has melted.

Page 83 1) Conductors.
2) Moving charged particles called electrons. 3) Static electricity.

Page 85 A fuse.

Page 87 1) True. 2) True.
3) False. Positive charges stick to negative charges.

Page 88 1) True. 2) True. 3) False. Hamster wheels are not connected to generators.

Page 90 1) Fossil fuels.
2) Deep underground.
3) A mine.

Page 95 1) True. 2) True. 3) False. When forces are balanced, an object stays at rest, or if it is moving, it keeps moving at a constant speed.

Page 97 1) True. 2) True. 3) True.

Page 99 1) False. Magnets have one north pole and one south pole. 2) True. 3) False. Aluminium is not magnetic.

Page 101 1) True. 2) False. Crows can't use levers. 3) True.

Page 102 1) Over a billion. 2) An internal combustion engine. 3) Petrol and diesel.

Page 105 1) It doesn't change – gravity is a constant force. 2) Acceleration. 3) The object will move at a constant speed or stay still.

Page 106 1) The wing shape pushes the air downwards. 2) Weight. 3) The tailplane keeps the plane stable.

Page 110 1) True. 2) False. We can only dig into the top layer of the Earth – the crust. 3) True.

Page 112 1) Seismometers.
2) The Richter scale.
3) Apart, together, and along.

Page 115 A drought.

Page 117 1) False. The largest ocean is the Pacific. 2) True. 3) True.

Page 119 1) Land heats up quicker than water. 2) A hurricane.

3) The Beaufort scale.

Page 121 1) Hurricanes need warm, moist air to develop. 2) The eye wall. 3) Winds need to reach at least 120 kph (73 mph) to be called a hurricane.

Page 122 1) True. 2) False. Other planets, such as Jupiter and Mercury, have an atmosphere. 3) True.

Page 125 Neil Armstrong.

Page 127 1) Venus.
2) Other planets outside our Solar System are too far away for us to travel to.
3) Exoplanets.

Page 129 1) True. 2) True. 3) False. Space is mainly empty.

Page 131 1) Space food is dry so it can last a long time. The water is added back into it in space. 2) The Russian space dog, Laika. 3) Rockets have to be powerful so they can escape the Earth's gravity.

Quiz your friends!

Who knows the most about science? Test your friends and family with these tricky questions. See pages 136–137 for the answers.

Questions

1. What is the name of the **chemical** in our **stomach** that **kills germs**?

6. In which state do materials have particles that are close together and in straight lines?

9. What kind of **electricity** makes our hair **stand on end?**

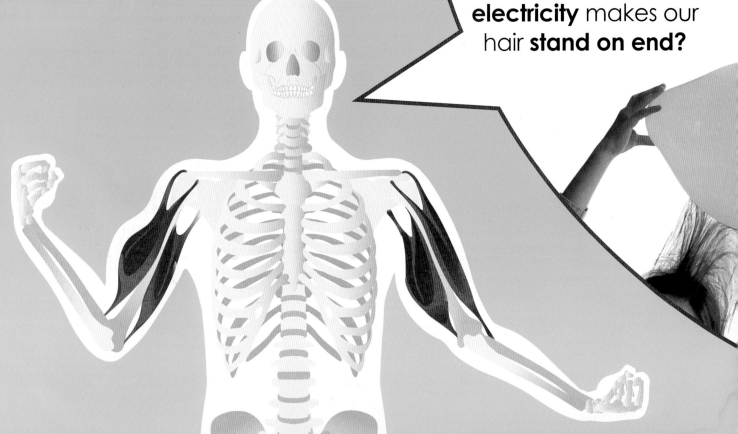

3. What is the **top layer of the skin** called?

4. What is the **smallest** living thing on Earth?

5. What are **feathers** made of?

2. How many different life stages does a **butterfly** go through?

7. What is the force that pulls us towards the Earth?

8. What is **litmus paper** used for?

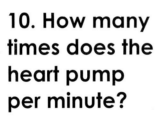

10. **How many times does the heart pump per minute?**

11. What is the name for a **mixture** of two or more **metals**?

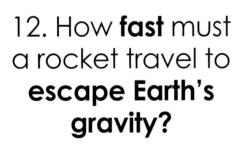

12. How **fast** must a rocket travel to **escape Earth's gravity?**

13. Where does **air** enter our **body**?

14. How much of the Earth's surface is covered in water?

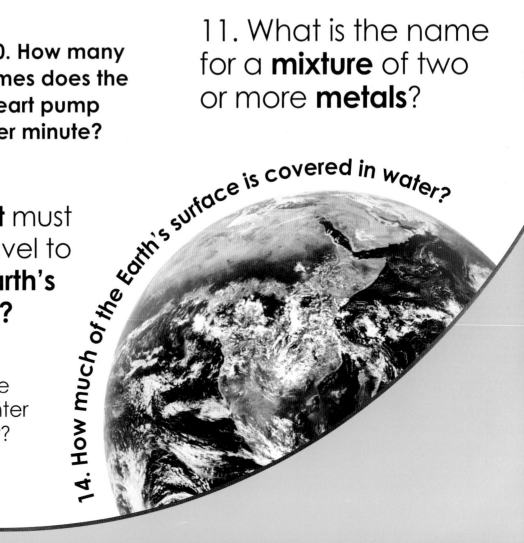

Answers

1. Hydrochloric acid

2. **Four**: egg, chrysalis pupa, butterfly

6. **Solid**

12. **40,000 kph (25,000 mph)** – that's 125 times faster than a racing car!

3. The **epidermis**

4. Bacteria

5. Keratin – the same material that **fingernails** are made of.

7. Gravity

8. Litmus paper is used to test how **acid** or **alkaline** a liquid is.

9. **Static electricity**

10. **The heart pumps blood around 80 times per minute.**

11. An alloy

14. Over **two-thirds**

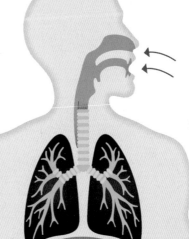

13. Through our **mouth** and **nose**

Glossary

Absorption
When something takes in another substance, for example, when a sponge absorbs liquid

Adaption
Way in which an animal or plant becomes better suited to its habitat

Amphibians
Cold-blooded vertebrates that start life in water before moving between land and water when grown

Archaeologist
Someone who looks for and studies ancient places and objects

Arteries
Tubes that carry blood rich in oxygen from the heart to the tissues

Arthropods
Group of vertebrates with a tough outer skeleton and a body divided into segments

Atoms
Smallest part of something that can take part in a chemical reaction

Bacteria
Tiny living things that can be found everywhere on Earth

Boundary
The point where one area ends and another begins

Camouflage
Colours or patterns that help something appear to blend in with its environment

Capillaries
Tiny blood vessel carrying blood through the tissues from arteries to veins

Cardiac
Of, or near, the heart

Cells
Tiny parts of the body that carry out different jobs, such as fighting infection

Cerebrum
Part of the brain involved in activities such as thinking, memory, movement, and sensation

Chrysalis
Hard casing a butterfly wraps itself in during metamorphosis

Circulatory
The system in the body made up of the heart and blood vessels

Conduction
When heat transfers between two things

Convection
When heat is transferred by the movement of fluids

Diaphragm
Muscle that moves up and down to control how much air is in your lungs

Evaporation
When a liquid is heated and changes into a gas or vapour

Exhale
To breathe out

Extracting
To take something away from something else

Filtration
When a liquid or gas is passed through something to remove small particles

Fluid
A gas or liquid

Force
Push or pull that causes things to start moving, to move faster, change direction, slow down, or stop moving

Fracture
A broken bone

Friction
Force created when two surfaces rub or slide against each other

Fuel
Substance that is burned to create heat or power

Inhale
To breathe in

Invertebrate
Animal that does not have a backbone

Keratin
A substance found in shells, claws, and skin

Lunar
Of the Moon

Malleable
An object or material that can be shaped without breaking

Mammals
Warm-blooded vertebrate animals that have skin covered in hair and feed their young milk

Material
Substance that can be used to make things. It can be natural or made by humans

Metamorphosis
Process by which some animals transform themselves into a different form from birth to adulthood

Minerals
Natural substances that grows in crystals, such as salt. All rocks are made from minerals

Molecules
Group of atoms bonded together

Mucus
A thick, sticky substance that protects the nose, lungs, and intestines

Muscle
Material in the body that contracts (shortens) to allow movement

Nerve
Long string of neurons carrying impulses between the brain, the spinal cord, and parts of the body

Neutron
A particle that has no charge

Nuclear
Being, or talking about, the nucleus of an atom

Nucleus
The central and most important part of an atom or cell

Orbit
Path an object takes when travelling around another object, when pulled by its gravity

Oxygen
Gas in the atmosphere that supports life

Particles
Extremely small parts of a solid, liquid, or gas

Photosynthesis
Process that green plants use to make food from sunlight

Pressure
Weight or force that is created when something is pressed against something else

Radiation
The transfer of energy through waves or particles. For example, heat from the Sun warming our faces

Reptiles
Cold-blooded vertebrates with scaly skin that usually reproduce by laying eggs

Solar
Word used to relate to the Sun and its energy

Spectrum
Range of something, for example, the range of colours in a rainbow

Streamlined
Something smooth that air can easily pass over

Telescope
Instrument used to look at distant objects

Vapour
Extremely small drops of liquid

Veins
Blood vessels that carry blood from the tissues towards the heart

Vertebrate
Animal that has a backbone

Vibration
Moving backwards and forwards small amounts very quickly

Index

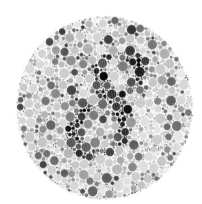

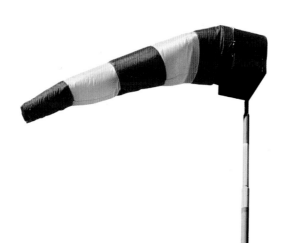

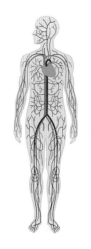

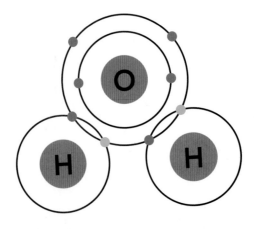

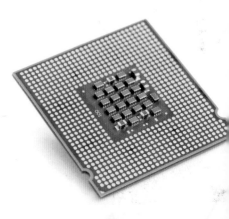

Acknowledgements

DORLING KINDERSLEY would like to thank Caroline Hunt for proofreading, and Helen Peters for the index. We would also like to thank Rhys Maddox, Alex Bailey, Scott Biggs, Rose McCloskey of the Fulbridge Academy Staff for consulting, and Dr Alec Bennett FRMetS, CMet for his help on the wind and hurricane pages.

The publisher would like to thank the following for their kind permission to reproduce their photographs:

(Key: a-above; b-below/bottom; c-centre; f-far; l-left; r-right; t-top)

2 Alamy Stock Photo: Kim Karpeles (cb). **Dreamstime.com:** Rob Stegmann / Geckophoto (crb). **3 Alamy Stock Photo:** Prisma Archivo (clb). **4 Dorling Kindersley:** Richard Leeney / Whipsnade Zoo (cra). **5 123RF.com:** Andrey Kryuchkov (cra); Steven Coling (ca); Fares Al Husseni (tr/Grass). **Depositphotos Inc:** Xalanx (tr). **7 Dreamstime.com:** Marcomayer (cra); Steven Melanson / Xscream1 (cr). **8 Dorling Kindersley:** Royal Tyrrell Museum of Palaeontology, Alberta, Canada (bl). **8-9 Dreamstime.com:** Steven Melanson / Xscream1 (t). **9 Dreamstime.com:** Wafuefotodesign (cr). **10-11 123RF.com:** Sergii Kolesnyk. **11 123RF.com:** Sebastian Kaulitzki (crb). **Getty Images:** David Shale / Nature Picture Library (br). **12 Dreamstime.com:** Iliuta Goean / Surub (bl); Rob Stegmann / Geckophoto (c). **12-13 Fotolia:** shama65 (c). **13 123RF.com:** Rafal Cichawa / rchphoto (cra). **Dreamstime.com:** Cathy Keifer / Cathykeifer (tc); Petergyure (cl); Wafuefotodesign (bc); Peter Wollinga (cr); Steven Melanson / Xscream1 (crb). **14 Alamy Stock Photo:** BSIP SA (cl). **Science Photo Library:** Dennis Kunkel Microscopy (clb). **15 Alamy Stock Photo. 16-17 Science Photo Library:** Nigel Cattlin (b). **17 123RF.com:** Maria Dryfhout (crb). **Alamy Stock Photo:** Nature Picture Library (bc). **Dorling Kindersley:** Claire Cordier (crb/Dandelion). **Dreamstime.com:** Dmitri Illarionov (cla). **18-19 naturepl.com:** Andy Sands. **18 123RF.com:** Chris Hill (bl); Tamara Kulikova (bc). **19 Science Photo Library:** Juergen Berger (cra). **20-21 Getty Images:** Karthik photography. **22 123RF.com:** T.W. Woodruff (bl). **Dorling Kindersley:** Natural History Museum, London (cra). **Dreamstime.com:** Alfredo Falcone (bc); Siloto (cr). **Science Photo Library:** Dennis Kunkel Microscopy (c). **22-23 Dorling Kindersley:** Richard Leeney / Whipsnade Zoo. **24-25 Depositphotos Inc:** Gudkovandrey. **24 Dreamstime.com:** Anke Van Wyk (crb). **25 Alamy Stock Photo:** Dominique Braud / Dembinsky Photo Associates (cra); Karen Debler (crb). **Depositphotos Inc:** enigma.art (cb). **Robert Harding Picture Library:** Philip Price (ca). **26-27 Getty Images:** Manoj Shah (b). **27 123RF.com:** edan (cla); Sergej Razvodovskij (ca). **28 Alamy Stock Photo:** SConcepts (bl). **29 123RF.com:** Ivan Martynyuk (cra). **Dreamstime.com:** Holger Leyrer / Leyrer (cr). **30 Science Photo Library:** Power and Syred (crb). **30-31 123RF.com:** Iakov Filimonov / jackf. **31 Alamy Stock Photo:** Florilegius (cra). **Dorling Kindersley:** Royal British Columbia Museum, Victoria, Canada (cr). **32-33 Dorling Kindersley:** Royal Tyrrell Museum of Palaeontology, Alberta, Canada. **33 Alamy Stock Photo:** Corbin17 (crb). **Dorling Kindersley:** Dan Crisp (ca). **Getty Images:** Scientifica (br). **34 Dorling Kindersley:** Arran Lewis (t). **34-35 Dreamstime.com:** Sebastian Kaulitzki / Eraxion (b). **35 Dreamstime.com:** Alexstar (t). **36 Science Photo Library:** Microscape (cr). **37 Dreamstime.com:** Sebastian Kaulitzki / Eraxion (cla). **Science Photo Library:** (ca). **40-41 Dorling Kindersley:** Arran Lewis. **40 Fotolia:** Yaumenenka / eAlisa (clb). **Getty Images:** Susumu Nishinaga (br). **43 123RF.com:** Oleg Mikhaylov (cla); Sergey Novikov (ca). **44 Dreamstime.com:** Karl Daniels / Webphoto99 (bl). **Getty Images:** Danita Delimont (clb). **46 Dreamstime.com:** Alexstar (clb); Sebastian Kaulitzki / Eraxion (bl). **49 Dreamstime.com:** Edvard Molnar / Edvard76 (cr). **52 Getty Images:** Image Source (bl). **53 123RF.com:** Suttha Burawonk (cla). **55 123RF.com:** didecs (cr). **Alamy Stock Photo:** Nir Alon (cra). **56 Dreamstime.com:** Christopher Wood / Chriswood44 (b). **56-57 Dreamstime.com:** Dmitry Islentyev (t). **57 Dreamstime.com:** Eugenesergeev (cr). **58 Alamy Stock Photo:** STOCKFOLIO® (clb); VIEW Pictures Ltd (bl). **60-61 123RF.com:** Gustavo Andrade. **61 Dreamstime.com:** Christopher Wood / Chriswood44 (ca); Pablo Hidalgo / Pxhidalgo (cra). **62-63 123RF.com:** Ksenia Ragozina. **65 Dorling Kindersley:** Booth Museum of Natural History (cra).

Dreamstime.com: Eugenesergeev (ca). **66-67 Getty Images:** Wakila. **68-69 Dreamstime.com:** Dmitry Islentyev (b). **69 Dreamstime.com:** Artem Gorohov / Agorohov (cla). **70-71 Dreamstime.com:** Maglara (b). **72 Dreamstime.com:** Lkordela (t). **72-73 iStockphoto.com:** KeithSzafranski (b). **73 123RF.com:** jezper (t). **74 iStockphoto.com:** KeithSzafranski. **75 Dreamstime.com:** Lkordela (cra); Meryll (cr). **76 Alamy Stock Photo:** Prisma Archivo (clb). **Getty Images:** mfto (cb). **79 Depositphotos Inc:** phakimata (r). **iStockphoto.com:** marshalgonz (cb). **80 Alamy Stock Photo:** Nature Picture Library (bl). **iStockphoto.com:** MarcelC (clb). **80-81 123RF.com:** Steven Coling. **82 123RF.com:** jezper (ca); skylightpictures (ca/Dam). **Dreamstime.com:** Dmitry Kalinovsky / Kadmy (cla). **82-83 123RF.com:** Pornkamol Sirimongkolpanich / ,inlovepai. **85 123RF.com:** cobalt (cra). **Dreamstime.com:** Leung Cho Pan (cr). **86 iStockphoto.com:** adventtr (bl); chargerv8 (clb). **87 Alamy Stock Photo:** Blend Images. **88 123RF.com:** nimon thong-uthai (cb). **Dreamstime.com:** Dan Van Den Broeke / Dvande (clb). **91 123RF.com:** adam88x (c). **Dreamstime.com:** Anankkml (cla). **92 Getty Images:** skodonnell (b). **92-93 123RF.com:** Cyoginan (t). **95 Dreamstime.com:** Stu Porter / Stuporter (cla). **96-97 Alamy Stock Photo:** Frank11. **98 123RF.com:** Cyoginan (clb). **100 Alamy Stock Photo:** John James Wood (clb). **101 123RF.com:** Anyka (clb). **Alamy Stock Photo:** Kim Karpeles (crb). **PunchStock:** Digital Vision / Martin Poole (ca). **103 Dreamstime.com:** Danil Roudenko / Danr13 (crb). **104-105 Getty Images:** skodonnell. **106-107 Alamy Stock Photo:** cmtransport. **Dreamstime.com:** Stevanzz (Sky). **107 Dorling Kindersley:** NASA (cra). **108 NASA and The Hubble Heritage Team (AURA/STScI):** NASA, ESA, and S. Beckwith (STScI) and the HUDF Team (tr). **NASA:** Bill Ingalls (b). **109 Dreamstime.com:** Seaphotoart (c). **110 123RF.com:** Andrey Kryuchkov (c/Grass and soil); Fares Al Husseni (c). **Depositphotos Inc:** Xalanx (cl). **111 Dreamstime.com:** Paul Van Den Berg / Paulvandenberg71 (ca). **112-113 Alamy Stock Photo:** Tawatchai Khid-arn. **114 Dreamstime.com:** Massimiliano Agati (bl). **115 Dreamstime.com:** Antonprado (cra). **117 Alamy Stock Photo:** Paulo Oliveira (br). **Dreamstime.com:** Seaphotoart (crb). **iStockphoto.com:** BulentBARIS (crb/Twilight). **118-119 123RF.com:** vacclav. **119 123RF.com:** Stanislav Pepeliaev (ca). **121 Dreamstime.com:** Lastdays1 (cla). **Getty Images:** Kevin Horan (ca). **122 Dreamstime.com:** Andrey Armyagov (tr). **123 Dreamstime.com:** Emmanuel Carabott / Emmanuelcarabott (clb); Lars Christensen / C-foto (crb); Ulkass (crb/Clouds). **NASA:** ESA, and the Hubble Heritage Team (STScI / AURA) (t). **124-125 Dreamstime.com:** Patryk Kosmider. **124 NASA:** (clb); ESA, and A. Simon (NASA Goddard) (cl). **125 Alamy Stock Photo:** Dennis Hallinan (crb). **127 NASA:** (ca); Ames / SETI Institute / JPL-Caltech (cla). **128-129 NASA and The Hubble Heritage Team (AURA/STScI):** NASA, ESA, and S. Beckwith (STScI) and the HUDF Team. **129 Dreamstime.com:** Tedsstudio (crb). **Getty Images:** Joe McNally (cr). **130 NASA:** (c, bc, br). **130-131 NASA:** Bill Ingalls. **133 Alamy Stock Photo:** cmtransport (clb). **134 Alamy Stock Photo:** Blend Images (crb). **135 Dreamstime.com:** Picstudio (ca). **Fotolia:** dundanim (crb). **iStockphoto.com:** thawats (tl). **136 Getty Images:** skodonnell (cl). **136-137 NASA:** Carla Cioffi (b). **137 Dorling Kindersley:** The Science Museum, London (c). **Dreamstime.com:** Andrey Sukhachev / Nchuprin (tr). **iStockphoto.com:** Tashatuvango (clb). **140 Dreamstime.com:** Andrey Armyagov (br). **Getty Images:** mfto (bc). **141 123RF.com:** Oleg Mikhaylov (bl); Stanislav Pepeliaev (bc); Sebastian Kaulitzki (bc/Water bear). **142 123RF.com:** didecs (br). **Dreamstime.com:** Leung Cho Pan (cb). **143 123RF.com:** Iakov Filimonov / jackf (br). **Dreamstime.com:** Iliuta Goean / Surub (cb).

Endpapers: Dreamstime.com: Irochka

Cover images: Front: 123RF.com: phive2015 cb; **Fotolia:** valdis torms clb; *Back:* **Alamy Stock Photo:** cmtransport cra; **Depositphotos Inc:** Gudkovandrey bl; **Dreamstime.com:** Gino Santa Maria tl, Leung Cho Pan cb, Patryk Kosmider tr

All other images © Dorling Kindersley
For further information see: www.dkimages.com